SOCIAL M___
In Business

SUCCEEDING IN THE
NEW INTERNET REVOLUTION

Steve Nicholls

SOCIAL MEDIA
In Business

SUCCEEDING IN THE
NEW INTERNET REVOLUTION

Steve Nicholls

Published by: Bookinars
5 Ruston Mews, London W11 1RB
www.Bookinars.co

Document title: Social Media In Business
Subtitle: Succeeding in the New Internet Revolution
ISBN: 978-1-908035-02-8
First edition: September 2011

Cover image credit: Rubik's Cube® used by permission of Seven Towns Ltd. www.rubiks.com

Trademarks
All brand names and product names referred to in this book are registered trademarks and unregistered trade names of their owners. The publisher and author are not connected with any of the products, services or vendors referred to in this book.

Disclaimers
This publication aims to provide accurate and reliable information regarding its subject matter covered. However, it is sold with the understanding that the author and publisher are not in their involvement with the book providing professional services/advice. The advice in this book may not be suitable for your business situation. The authors and publishers specifically disclaim any liability arising from the use or application of the contents of the book. You should consult a professional where appropriate.

Visit our website at: www.SocialMediaInBusiness.com

Dedication

I would like to dedicate this book to Vinod Chaudhry, Peter Goodwin, Fiona Young, Mary Howgate, and Zalia Esslinger for supporting the book and for helping me in ways that truly touched my heart.

Acknowledgments

FIRST, I WANT TO ACKNOWLEDGE YOU THE READER for investing your time and money to study this book. In all seriousness, 80% of success in any field is turning up; thank you for turning up.

I wish to thank Vinod Chaudhry, my good friend, for mentoring me through my MSc and for assisting me with this book that flowed from the MSc process. To Peter Goodwin, for being a good friend, for contributing to the development of the project management section, and for his sound advice throughout the process.

I would also like to thank Hitendra Patel, James Kilgarriff, Steve Lowe, Ichiko Sopp, Greg Malpass, Khatia Krebs, Keoki Trask, Noboru Yamamoto, Anthony DelGreco, Paul Miller, Fiona Young, Mary Howgate, Jean McDoniels, George Kedourie, and Alun Richards for their friendship and support. A special mention is made to T. Harv Eker, Blair Singer, Larry Gilman, John Kehoe, and Alex Mandossian for their training and for inspiring me to finally write this book.

Thanks to Jefferson Pacaman and Simon Laughton for drafting the diagrams and to xkcd.com for the excellent overview of the social media landscape graphics. My appreciation also goes to Erdenebulgan Tsogbadrakh for the initial cover concept, to Simon Butterfield for the *Social Media In Business* logo design, and to Alison Rayner for the typesetting and page layout.

All Rubik's Cube® images used by permission of Seven Towns Ltd. (www.rubiks.com).

My gratitude also goes to Janis Cox Millett for the final draft editing, and to Rod Romesburg, Monica Guy, Zalia Esslinger, and Penny Clark for editing and proofreading the preliminary versions.

Finally, thanks to the industry professionals who kindly gave up their time to take part in the survey and provided their views on the subject matter.

Thank you.
Steve

Before you turn another page...

Have you ever purchased a book,
read it, and then ended up
with more questions than answers?

Not any more.
Ask me anything about the book,
and I will answer the most frequently
asked questions submitted to the website
"live" as part of a Q&A session:

www.AskSteve.co

For additional information go to:
www.SocialMediaInBusiness.com/Tools

Table of Contents

TABLE OF FIGURES (AND TABLES)...*10*

PREFACE..*12*

EXECUTIVE BRIEFING *15*

ABOUT THIS BOOK...*20*

Chapter 1 – Four Business Opportunities *30*

1.1   **INTRODUCTION** *26*

1.2   **VISIBLE MARKET PRESENCE** *29*

     1.2.1   Search Engine Visibility *30*

     1.2.2   Global Reach *32*

     1.2.3   CASE STUDY: Local and Global Example – Groupon.com *33*

1.3   **COMMUNICATION**..*35*

     1.3.1   Internal versus External Communication.............................*36*

     1.3.2   Formal versus Informal Communication *37*

     1.3.3   An Example of Using Social Media for Reaching Out to Customers *40*

     1.3.4   CASE STUDY: Communication Example – Socialmedia.Cisco.com *41*

1.4   **COMMUNITIES**..*43*

     1.4.1   Relationships Mapping *45*

     1.4.2   Social Capital *46*

     1.4.3   Six Degrees of Separation...*48*

     1.4.4   CASE STUDY: Communities Example – LinkedIn.com..............*49*

1.5   **COLLECTIVE INTELLIGENCE**...*52*

     1.5.1   CASE STUDY: Collective Intelligence Example – My Starbucks Idea *56*

1.6   **COLLABORATION**...*57*

     1.6.1   Internal Collaboration *59*

     1.6.2   External Collaboration *60*

     1.6.3   CASE STUDY: Collaboration Example – Accenture *61*

1.7   **TAKE AWAY POINTS** *63*

Chapter 2 – Social Media Development *65*

2.1   **EVOLUTION OF THE INTERNET** *66*

2.2   **THE CHANGING SOCIAL MEDIA LANDSCAPE**.....................*69*

2.3   **RISE OF MOBILITY**..*72*

     2.3.1   Augmented Reality on Mobiles *74*

     2.3.2   Rise of QR Codes and Microsoft Tags *75*

2.4   **RISE OF CLOUD COMPUTING** *76*

2.5   **RISE OF INTERNET ON OUR TELEVISION SCREENS**..................*78*

SocialMediaInBusiness.com

2.6   INSIGHTS FROM SOCIAL MEDIA USERS 79

   2.6.1   Overview *80*

   2.6.2   Increase Visible Market Presence *81*

   2.6.3   Learning by Remote Training and Study *82*

   2.6.4   Product Creation *82*

   2.6.5   Enhancing Personal Reputation and Social Capital *83*

   2.6.6   Relationship Building and Linking for Information and Expertise *83*

   2.6.7   Recruitment, Resourcing, and Sourcing *84*

   2.6.8   Keeping in Touch with Colleagues and Reconnecting
          with Past Contacts *84*

   2.6.9   Project Collaboration *84*

   2.6.10 Being One Step Ahead of Formal Communication *85*

   2.6.11 Benefits of Social Networks over Intranets for Internal Communication ...*85*

2.7   TAKE AWAY POINTS *87*

Chapter 3 – Social Media Applications Guide 91

3.1   COMMUNICATION *93*

   3.1.1   Meetings and Conferencing *94*

   3.1.2   Media Sharing *96*

   3.1.3   Location Services *97*

   3.1.4   Broadcasting *98*

3.2   COMMUNITIES *100*

   3.2.1   Marketplaces *101*

   3.2.2   Social Networks *102*

   3.2.3   Blogs and Microblogs *104*

   3.2.4   Virtual Worlds *106*

3.3   COLLABORATION *108*

   3.3.1   Freelance Platforms *108*

   3.3.2   Project and Team *111*

   3.3.3   DIY Wiki Platforms *112*

   3.3.4   DIY Social Networks *113*

3.4   COLLECTIVE INTELLIGENCE *115*

   3.4.1   Discussion Sites *115*

   3.4.2   Wikis *117*

   3.4.3   Ideas Platforms *118*

   3.4.4   Market Intelligence *120*

3.5   TAKE AWAY POINTS *122*

Chapter 4 – Social Media: The Dark Side 123

4.1   INTRODUCTION *124*

AskSteve.co

4.2   THE OVERLAP OF PERSONAL AND PROFESSIONAL LIFE 124
4.3   TOP FIVE CHALLENGES FROM AN ORGANIZATION'S PERSPECTIVE . . 127
    4.3.1   Reputation Management 128
    4.3.2   Security – Hacking, Spy-ware, Bugs... 129
    4.3.3   Engaging in Dialogue and Conversation 130
    4.3.4   Trust as Part of the Culture 130
    4.3.5   Wasting Company Time 130
4.4   TOP FIVE CHALLENGES FROM INDIVIDUALS' PERSPECTIVES 130
    4.4.1   Lack of Time 130
    4.4.2   Company Spying and Permanent Storage of Web Activities 132
    4.4.3   Maintaining Privacy 132
    4.4.4   Trust and Misrepresentation 133
    4.4.5   Identity Management 133
    4.4.6   The Impact on the Business 134
4.5   "DARK SIDE" MITIGATION STRATEGIES 138
    4.5.1   Consider Social Media as Part of Your Strategic Planning Process . . 140
    4.5.2   Have Clear Social Media Policies 141
    4.5.3   Tools 144
    4.5.4   Training and Development 144
    4.5.5   Mindset and Culture 145
    4.5.6   Fostering a Relationship of Trust 146
4.6   TAKE AWAY POINTS 147

Chapter 5 – 3-CORE Project Success System 149
5.1   INTRODUCTION 150
5.2   PART 1 – BUSINESS ENVIRONMENT 152
    5.2.1   Project Pitfalls to Avoid 154
5.3   PART 2 – PROJECT STAGES 156
    5.3.1   Briefing Stage 157
    5.3.2   Project Definition Stage 157
    5.3.3   Project Planning Stage 160
    5.3.4   Project Implementation Stage 162
    5.3.5   Project Roll-out Stage 163
5.4   TAKE AWAY POINTS 165

Chapter 6 – Project Development Cycle 167
6.1   GOALS 169
6.2   ANALYSIS 172
6.3   PROJECTS 174
6.4   STRATEGY 177

SocialMediaInBusiness.com

6.5   ACTIONS 180
6.6   MEASURE 181
6.7   COMMUNICATION 184
6.8   TIME-OUTS – IMPORTANCE OF TIME INTERVALS
      BETWEEN DEVELOPMENT CYCLES 188
6.9   TAKE AWAY POINTS 190

Chapter 7 – The Project Development Cycle in Action 193

7.1   CASE STUDY: BOOK PROJECT – THE BRIEFING STAGE 194
7.2   CASE STUDY: BOOK PROJECT – PROJECT DEFINITION STAGE ... 197
7.3   CASE STUDY: BOOK PROJECT – PROJECT PLANNING STAGE 198
      7.3.1   Goals 198
      7.3.2   Analysis 199
      7.3.3   Projects 200
      7.3.4   Strategy 203
      7.3.5   Actions 204
      7.3.6   Measure 207
      7.3.7   Communication 209
7.4   CASE STUDY: FINAL THOUGHTS 210

Chapter 8 – Next Steps 211

8.1   HOW DO YOU GET STARTED WITH SOCIAL MEDIA
      IN YOUR ORGANIZATION? 212
8.2   WHAT ARE THE TYPICAL OBSTACLES THAT
      PREVENT PEOPLE FROM GETTING STARTED? 214
      8.2.1   A Need for a Common Language 214
      8.2.2   Social Media is Not Just About Facebook, Twitter, YouTube, and LinkedIn . 215
      8.2.3   Differing Mindsets and Perceptions 216
      8.2.4   Social Media is Not Free 216
      8.2.5   Deal with the Security Issues 217
      8.2.6   Visible and Invisible Impacts on the Business .. 217
      8.2.7   The Balance of Power Between Organization and Individual 218
8.3   WHAT ARE THE STRATEGIES THAT OVERCOME THESE OBSTACLES? .. 218
8.4   WHAT IS THE FIRST STEP TO GETTING STARTED? 219

REFERENCES 222
FURTHER READING 226
ABOUT THE AUTHOR 227
GLOSSARY 228
INDEX 234

AskSteve.co

Table of Figures

Figure 1 – Social Media Overwhelm *20*

Figure 2 – Four Business Opportunities *27*

Figure 3 – Global Reach and New Markets *29*

Figure 4 – Google Search Ranking (PR0-10) *30*

Figure 5 – Percentage of Clicks by Position (www.seobook.com) *31*

Figure 6 – Communication *35*

Figure 7 – A Promotion Where You Can Become a SuperFan of Cisco
            and Highlighted on Their Facebook Page *42*

Figure 8 – Communities of Interest *44*

Figure 9 – Social Network Analysis (Cross, Nohria & Parker, 2002) *45*

Figure 10 – Six Degrees of Separation – Stanley Milgram *48*

Figure 11 – Collective Intelligence *52*

Figure 12 – Collaboration Model for Competitive Advantage *57*

Figure 13 – Web 2.0 Meme Map *67*

Figure 14 – Internet, the Giant Computer *68*

Figure 15 – Social Media Landscape 2007 – by Randall Munroe (www.xkcd.com) . . .*70*

Figure 16 – Social Media Landscape 2010 – by Randall Munroe (www.xkcd.com) . . .*71*

Figure 17 – Mobility: Smartphones and Tablet Computers *73*

Figure 18 – Scan QR Code or Microsoft Tag for www.smqrcode.com *75*

Figure 19 – Rise of Cloud Computing *77*

Figure 20 – Social Media Applications Guide *93*

Figure 21 – A Sample of Communication Applications *94*

Figure 22 – A Sample of Communities Applications *100*

Figure 23 – A Sample of Collaboration Applications *109*

Figure 24 – A Sample of Collective Intelligence Applications *115*

Figure 25 – The Overlap of Professional and Personal Lives *125*

Figure 26 – The Smartphone and iPad Mobile Devices *126*

Figure 27 – Social Media Breaks *127*

Figure 28 – Top Five Risks and Challenges *128*

Figure 29 – The Importance of Visible and Invisible Impacts on a Business *134*

Figure 30 – Five Mitigation Strategies *140*

SocialMediaInBusiness.com

Figure 31 – The 3-CORE Project Success System...................................... *151*

Figure 32 – The Business Environment: Pitfalls and Constraints *152*

Figure 33 – Project Stages *156*

Figure 34 – Real-World Implementation is a Vector *162*

Figure 35 – Roll-out Stage *164*

Figure 36 – The Project Development Cycle..................................... *168*

Figure 37 – Goals Hierarchy... *169*

Figure 38 – Analysis Lens – Snapshot... *172*

Figure 39 – Social Media Project Design *174*

Figure 40 – Three Levels of a Product *176*

Figure 41 – Social Media Strategy.. *177*

Figure 42 – Actions to Achieve the Milestones *180*

Figure 43 – Measure – Social Media Aspect of the Project..................... *182*

Figure 44 – Project Stages and the Changing Business Environment *183*

Figure 45 – Before and After Analysis.. *183*

Figure 46 – Communication – ABC – Always Be Communicating................ *185*

Figure 47 – Importance of Time-outs *189*

Figure 48 – Post-it Project Development Cycle Meeting........................ *195*

Figure 49 – Second Project Development Cycle................................. *198*

Figure 50 – Social Media Symbol *199*

Figure 51 – Book Launch Model *201*

Figure 52 – Timeline for Launching the Book *203*

Tables

Table 1 – Social Media Sites with Most Traffic, 2007–2010...................... *69*

Table 2 – Sixteen Application Categories *92*

Table 3 – Sixteen Categories of Social Media and 32 Examples................ *122*

Table 4 – Project Pitfalls and Solutions..................................... *155*

Table 5 – Increasing Cost of Hidden Issues *162*

Table 6 – Measures for the Book Launch *208*

AskSteve.co

Preface

One thing I have learned in many years of working with technologies of all kinds: technology moves faster than people and people move faster than companies. So we see with social media. It is so much more popular in the personal than in the business space. This is changing, however, where businesses in general, with some notable exceptions, have been slow to respond to the social media opportunities.

A friend who is a corporate executive of a large international company recently revealed that in his organization Facebook, Twitter, and most popular social media applications are banned! He wore it as a badge of honor that social media is not for companies: it is for kids and for playing games. Ironically, his daughter is launching an Internet company using social media as the primary marketing channels.

Most of the clients I visited said, "Yes, we know about social media. We have got Facebook, Twitter, YouTube, and LinkedIn." This is great, but upon a closer look they are not really doing a whole lot with them. Why? Because there is often no rationale behind what they are doing.

Jargon and low-level data surround social media, often creating confusion. It is important to have a common language so that we can understand the difference between data and strategic information. 90% of the data thrown at us is meaningless unless it is in context and translated into a language we all understand.

Organizational problems are really cleverly disguised people issues. Social media is a people issue; the technology is the enabler. The attitudes and beliefs of people will be more important than the technical issues.

The great news for business owners, managers, and leaders of companies is that social media is not difficult to learn, but we need to have a good framework or model for what it is all about.

In writing this book, I wanted to achieve the following:

- Provide a simple framework to help you as a manager or business leader to understand the opportunities presented by social media and to enable you

SocialMediaInBusiness.com

to create a common language of what social media means for your whole organization.

- Present an overview of the potential risks and impact of social media on your organization in a broader strategic sense and show how they can be addressed.

- Present a practical framework for the introduction and implementation of social media projects that require mindset changes in the organization and, as such can often come up against serious resistance. This I have called The 3-CORE Project Success System. It is a tool I have developed over many years and is very flexible and effective.

Have no doubt: this is a revolution. New companies like Groupon are using social media to create completely new business models that would not be possible without it.

The aim, therefore, is that this book enables you to excel with your social media projects, so as to make your organization more successful.

An example of the potential the new technology offers: to provide mass customization to their customers, Coca-Cola's "Freestyle" vending machine is being used to mix the exact flavor that an individual wants from more than 100 options. The machine also transmits supply and demand information to Coca-Cola's main office, providing business intelligence that can be used to develop new products; show popular locations, peak times, and popular flavors; and give insight by location on what customers like. Customers can share their drink mix with their friends using social media.

Another new arena is in the mobile field. According to Gartner, in 2011 there were 17.7 billion mobile applications generating $15 billion. Their prediction is for 21.6 billion to be sold for a total of $29.5 billion in 2013. None of this existed before the launch of the Apple iPhone in June 2007.

And as we can see from the news channels, dictators in Middle Eastern countries, such as Tunisia and Egypt, have not been able to stop the spread through social media of "people power." It will be the same for our organizations. We have to embrace social media because we can not stop it.

AskSteve.co

Your customers, competitors, and suppliers are to varying degrees angling to gain an advantage through social media. From finding a partner on a dating site, to getting advice on a hotel from TripAdvisor, to solving complex problems (as NASA has done using competitions), social media has become an increasingly dominant force.

In my view, this is not a choice any more. It is a strategic resource and a new dimension to corporate strategy. My advice is simple: embrace the new Internet revolution before your competitors figure it out, because this is not something you can respond to by buying a new machine or hiring a specialist. It takes time to bring your employees up to speed. It will take time to come to terms with and achieve meaningful results.

My name is Steve Nicholls. I am not a PR or advertising agency guru, technical genius, or marketing manager for a well-known brand. Unless we have met, you are probably wondering who I am!

Many years ago I used to help build skyscrapers in the construction industry as a project manager. I then studied for an MBA and changed careers completely into the telecommunications sector, working for a large UK telecom company. It was a quite a culture shock, I can tell you!

Since then, I've worked for a number of successful startup and growth companies in the telecoms and Internet space before setting up my own consulting company focusing on software implementation and training. In essence, I am a business person who has learned social media during my career in telecoms, in the days when dial-up modems were all we had to access the Internet.

This book has been quite a journey for me. I revisited this fascinating subject that I researched back in 2008 for an MSc project. In looking to update it three years later with the intention of publishing it, I had to totally rewrite it, as the Internet landscape has changed so completely in that time and is still changing.

I hope you find this subject as fascinating as I do and hope your journey into this exciting new landscape will be as rewarding as mine.

SocialMediaInBusiness.com

Executive Briefing

Social Media In Business discusses both the business opportunities of social media and the pitfalls to avoid. Above all, it shows how to put it all into practice. No matter what the starting point for an individual or business, whether a complete novice with social media or a manager with several applications already in use, the chapters of this book lay out a compelling case for managers to bring social media to the forefront of their business strategy.

Chapter 1 presents the four must-have social media opportunities available to businesses today: Communication, Communities, Collective Intelligence, and Collaboration.

In order to take advantage of these opportunities, managers must implement a comprehensive social media strategy that complies with organizational policies, as well as sales and marketing plans. This will allow the company to reap the greatest benefits while avoiding the pitfalls of social media platforms.

Despite the opportunities readily available, social media is not a panacea – the rules of business still apply. Managers must be aware that the benefits derived from using social media are profoundly influenced by culture, power structure, and politics.

Chapter 2 explains the evolution of the Internet and developments in the arena of social media – what the technologies and software applications look like and how they can best serve a business.

The Internet landscape has drastically changed. As recently as 2008 the most popular application was MySpace; three years later, Facebook is the most popular social network. The fast-changing social media landscape means that managers have to keep an eye on this industry to understand how it is evolving. This will allow organizations to adapt their business procedures to match the changing ways that people interact with social media.

The Internet, however, is not free. There are two costs: time and the cost incurred in maintenance and training that may impact the benefits you gain from social media. This

AskSteve.co

is why unconventional, innovative thinking is required to find that perfect combination of tools and strategies in order to achieve the most out of social media.

Chapter 3 categorizes and then describes in some detail a range of specific social media applications.

Given how quickly the field of social media has exploded onto the scene, it is no surprise that the possibilities can seem overwhelming. Using the four key business opportunities explained earlier, it is possible to narrow the field to sixteen widely-available applications or tools that businesses can easily use to their advantage.

Chapter 4 alerts readers to social media's "dark side." It lays out a set of five well-known risks and challenges to an organization and then describes mitigation techniques to counter these.

There are some rather delicate issues that need to be managed and balanced between the individual and the organization. The top five risks and challenges are:

Organization's Perspective:

- Reputation management
- Security – hacking, spy-ware, bugs, etc.
- Engaging in dialogue and conversation
- Trust as part of the culture
- Wasting company time

Individual's Perspective:

- Lack of time
- Company spying and permanent storage of online conduct
- Maintaining privacy
- Trust and misrepresentation
- Identity management

Five Mitigation Strategies

- Business Planning
- Social Media Policy
- Training Program
- Mindset and Culture
- Relationship of Trust

SocialMediaInBusiness.com

Chapter 5 introduces The 3-CORE Project Success System. Setting out the work of developing social media in the context of an organization's business environment, it shows how project stages can be used to develop a program for social media.

As you define your social media goals and move toward their implementation in your organization, it is important to remember the broader organizational context in which social media will be used. This will ensure that your social media goals align with the broader business goals.

Chapter 6 presents the seven steps to implement a project: the Project Development Cycle. The use of this practical tool for implementing change in any business is shown with the example of a social media project within the context of a business with existing project procedures.

The Project Development Cycle for planning and implementing social media projects can enable an organization to achieve optimum social media success. The steps of the Project Development Cycle are straightforward and logical, yet flexible enough to fit your organization's best way of doing business.

It is an iterative learning process where each experience is used for the next cycle, with each turn of the wheel adding greater depth of insight. Time gaps between planning cycles allow for a deeper understanding of the project requirements, time for reflection, and time to gather additional information.

Chapter 7 offers the real-life story of the Project Development Cycle in action to implement social media applications.

Chapter 8 proposes a solid starting point for achieving a successful social media project.

This chapter lays down several key steps and reveals typical obstacles and strategies to overcome these. It suggests that the first step to getting started is the briefing stage to define the potential program.

AskSteve.co

INTRODUCTION

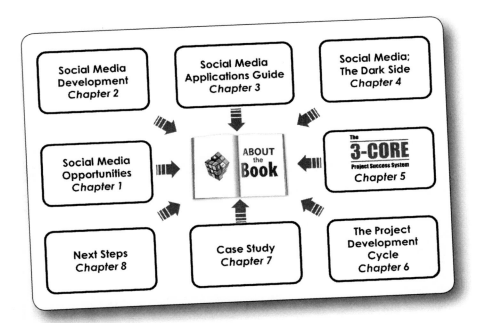

About This Book

About this book…

What is social media?

THE PHENOMENON OF SOCIAL MEDIA has arisen from the simple concept of users generating and sharing content. There are no precise definitions, and it can be overwhelming and confusing to understand. Social media is a generic label given to describe the dynamic interaction among the entire global community, enabled by the use of web-based and mobile technological advancements. In fact, social media and Internet are now readily interchangeable terms (sometimes it is called Web 2.0, 3.0, Web Squared, or just the Internet).

FIGURE 1 • *Social Media Overwhelm*

Why is social media so important?

Social media is so important because it represents a major shift in the way the Internet is being used by you, your customers, competitors, and suppliers…in fact by everyone. The main shift is in the way people in cyberspace actively participate and interact with people, rather than just viewing pages. It has kind of sneaked up on everyone and represents an ongoing evolution of the Internet, helped by technology (with new

SocialMediaInBusiness.com

devices such as: smartphones, tablet computers, Internet on flat screen televisions), communication companies (increasing access to broadband technology), and new media companies (with new applications like Facebook). We now have access to tools that mean we can do a whole range of things that used to be only available to a select few (e.g. broadcasting). This has not happened overnight; it started out mainly in the consumer area with social activities like dating, gaming, and social networking applications, to name a few. If you are one of those people that thought this was for having fun, you are right. However, all businesses are now embracing it. You will have to as well because your customers and competitors already are... no longer is it a choice.

What are the key aims of this book?

1. To provide a clear guide to social media in business for managers

This book aims to help the manager to understand the opportunities and to create a common language of what social media means for your whole organization, not just the marketing and information technology (IT) parts of the business that tend to dominate the conversation around social media. Secondly, it provides a guide to a host of available social media applications and tools for business. Finally, the book presents an overview of the potential risks and impact of social media on your organization in a broader strategic sense.

2. To provide a practical framework for the introduction and implementation of social media that can be adapted to your organization – The 3-CORE Project Success System

The framework introduced in this book is **The 3-CORE Project Success System**, based on three elements: Business Environment, Project Stages, and The Project Development Cycle. The key idea is that the framework can be adapted to your organizational context and is easy to use in training employees who may not be familiar with social media or project management. The Project Development Cycle is a tool developed by the author to help organizations meet the above objectives.

It is important to note, this is not a "how-to" manual for using Facebook or Twitter. There are plenty of existing resources that are recommended on the accompanying website: www.SocialMediaInBusiness.com.

AskSteve.co

Who is this book for?

As the title suggests, this book was written for business owners, managers, and policy-makers. It is particularly relevant to those who operate in the business-to-business sector and those who are eager to exploit current technologies in order to increase the competitiveness of their organizations. This book is designed to help managers develop an implementation strategy, as well as to help them shift their mindset in order to effectively integrate social media into their business processes.

IN *SOCIAL MEDIA IN BUSINESS*, READERS WILL DISCOVER:

- Four Business Opportunities of Social Media
- How Social Media has Developed over the Last Three Years
- The Social Media Applications Guide
- Five Social Media "Dark Sides" and Mitigation Strategies
- The 3-CORE Project Success System
- The Project Development Cycle

What is in the book?

Social Media In Business discusses both the business advantages of social media and the pitfalls to avoid; and shows how to put it all into practice. No matter what the starting point for an individual or business, whether a complete novice with social media or a manager with several applications already in use, the reader will learn:

Chapter 1: The four must-have social media opportunities available to businesses

Chapter 2: The social media developments – what they look like and how they can best serve a business

Chapter 3: Details of social media applications to enable users to understand the types of applications that are available and their benefits

Chapter 4: The Social Media Dark Side – the risks and challenges to an organization and mitigation techniques to counter these risks

SocialMediaInBusiness.com

Chapter 5: Guiding principles for implementing social media tools in your organization

Chapter 6: The Project Development Cycle, an easy-to-use and practical tool for implementing change in any business

Chapter 7: A real-life story of the Project Development Cycle in action to implement social media applications

Chapter 8: Next Steps

How can you get the most from this book?

Start with an open mind.

Social media by its nature is experiential, and experience is highly subjective. Most people's experience with social media is going to be quite different, depending on the context and what they already know. In other words, we all have some preconceived ideas about social media. Effectively learning something new is more often than not about unlearning what we already know.

The idea of starting with an open mind is to purposely set aside all that you know when you begin and allow yourself the space to learn something new. The poem by John Godfrey Saxe, from the mid-1800s, highlights the dilemma:

The Essence of an Elephant

It was six men of Indostan, to learning much inclined, who went to see the Elephant (though all of them were blind), that each by observation might satisfy his mind.

The First approached the Elephant, and happening to fall against his broad and sturdy side, at once began to bawl: "God bless me! But the Elephant is very like a wall!"

The Second, feeling of the tusk cried, "Ho! What have we here, so very round and smooth and sharp? To me it is mighty clear this wonder of an Elephant is very like a spear!"

AskSteve.co

The Third approached the animal, and happening to take the squirming trunk within his hands, thus boldly up he speak: "I see," quote he, "the Elephant is very like a snake!"

The Fourth reached out an eager hand, and felt about the knee: "What most this wondrous beast is like is mighty plain," quote he. "It is clear enough the Elephant is very like a tree!"

The Fifth, who chanced to touch the ear, said: "Even the blindest man can tell what this resembles most; Deny the fact who can, this marvel of an Elephant is very like a fan!"

The Sixth no sooner had begun about the beast to grope, than, seizing on the swinging tail that fell within his scope. "I see," quote he, "the Elephant is very like a rope!"

And so these men of Indostan disputed loud and long, each in his own opinion exceeding stiff and strong, though each was partly in the right and all were in the wrong!

John Godfrey Saxe (1816–1887)

John Saxe's poem describes how, if we were one of those blind men and we stopped after the first visit to the elephant, we would go away with a narrow experience of the elephant and be fixed at our limited understanding. Social media is a bit like that: there is a world of difference between the much focused-upon application tools (Facebook, Twitter, and YouTube etc.) and the integration of social media into the fabric of your business. You must understand the risks and opportunities and design a step-by-step method of implementation. This is the challenge being faced by many business owners, managers, and policy-makers today, and this book is your guide to help you do it in a unique way for your particular business.

You are invited to approach the subject of social media with an open mind and try some of the ideas, keep what you like, and discard or change the rest to make it your own system.

CHAPTER 1

• • • • •

Four Business Opportunities

1.1 **Introduction**

SOCIAL MEDIA APPLICATIONS ON THE INTERNET contribute a variety of new opportunities to people and organizations. To businesses, they offer access to the global market by providing the user with worldwide visibility. The most basic opportunity afforded to organizations is the ability to communicate on a much wider scale on all fronts of the business: inter-office, between lower and upper management, within special groups or planning teams, and with customers, suppliers, or potential business partners literally all over the globe. Businesses can now access, create, and develop whole communities of interest, on both local and global scales. Additionally, organizations can tap into collective intelligence, collecting various viewpoints from inside and outside the organization to consider in critical decision-making. Social media enables collaboration with independent experts or teams through online communities or virtual meetings, often resulting in better-quality input, increased productivity, and greater efficiency. Lastly, these applications provide a means to identify, measure, and monitor social capital (the value of a network), supplying ways in which businesses may maximize their network's potential value.

In order to gain competitive advantage in one's given industry, business managers often have to employ innovative methods. Exploiting social media for business is an example of one such unconventional practice. Though social media venues are widely used now by individuals, their application in the professional environment is less widespread. Within corporations, internal channels like intranets and other databases are not always linked to external online technologies. This is partly due to the real fear of security breaches and loss of control. However, when considering the opportunities and benefits businesses can gain from using social media, management must ask if they can afford to ignore them in today's marketplace. Businesses are now seizing the opportunities created by social media functions and have joined online platforms such as Facebook, Twitter, YouTube, and LinkedIn. These businesses realize that social media offers much more than basic social networking, as this book explains.

The topic of social media is presented here with the intent of providing guidance for managers on how to harness the power of communication to grow their business.

SocialMediainBusiness.com

Throughout this chapter, the nature of the four opportunities is detailed in sections, and at the end of each section an illustrative example is given of an organization known to have benefited. At the end of the chapter, take away points and action guides are provided.

FIGURE 2 • *Four Business Opportunities*

The Goal: Visible Market Presence – It goes without saying that advertising in local offline media outlets is an avenue for increasing visibility in one's industry. However, an online presence for your business offers the type of visibility that only the Internet is capable of providing. Social media can provide worldwide access to your business, allowing increased visibility and making it possible to be "present in the global marketplace." The global market also encompasses the specific local market niches within which a company operates. However, social media removes any limitations of a business's potential reach. Increased visibility is one of the benefits of using social media tools.

AskSteve.co

These tools provide the following opportunities for businesses to increase their presence on the worldwide stage:

1. **Communication** – Social media offers tools to enhance communication between management staff, employees, customers, and suppliers. The result is an increase in and development of *conversations* and *relationships* that can enhance productivity, efficiency, and loyalty.

2. **Communities** – Social media can create and provide access to communities of interest for a business. These are your markets. This in turn increases awareness of the company, helps to brand the business, and builds overall trust. In doing so, communities provide *increased social capital* to the business.

3. **Collective Intelligence** – Social media can provide access to a massive pool of independent thinkers, both inside and outside the organization, to help management *access a wide variety of ideas* and reach the best decisions. This can save time, money, and other limited company resources.

4. **Collaboration** – Social media can create high-performance teams by facilitating collaboration amongst individual experts at many different levels. It creates effective working partnerships between staff, department heads, upper management, sister organizations, and the wider stakeholders of a company.

There are a lot of overlaps between the four opportunities within the global marketplace. However, for the purposes of this writing, the list of opportunities is merely a guide. Most real world social media platforms have elements of each opportunity built into the application's function. Managers are only limited by the extent to which they understand the different applications and the benefits that they offer. The ability to learn how to extract benefits from available tools will determine a business's readiness for future technological applications.

• • • • •

SocialMediaInBusiness.com

1.2 **Visible Market Presence**

FIGURE 3 • *Global Reach and New Markets*

GLOBAL MARKET ACCESS is the direct result of having a visible online presence. It is especially advantageous for the parts of your organization that interact with customers directly, such as the marketing, sales, business development, and customer service departments. There is simply no better way for your organization to gain access to the most customers, clients, and potential partners over the widest part of the market at the greatest speed and at the lowest cost. Social media platforms can help to increase the efficiency of all the value-creating functions in your organization. Businesses can access the global and local niche markets to sell products and services, and to source information on other organizations' products, services, and expertise. This information can be especially useful for reducing costs and taking advantage of the four business opportunities that social media offers.

AskSteve.co

Social media marketing fits into the broader category of Internet marketing. It includes key areas such as: market research, web optimization, traffic building, traffic conversion, product creation, customer support, blogging, and search engine optimization. These will be discussed in more detail in the chapters to follow.

1.2.1 Search Engine Visibility

In order to capitalize on the many benefits of the Internet, organizations need to be extremely visible on any search engine, but especially the world's leader: Google (www.google.com). Websites are positioned and ranked according to popularity and traffic received (see Figure 4). Google is by far the largest information search engine and is second only to Facebook (www.facebook.com) in terms of traffic (as of May 2011).

The main objective of organizations hoping to grow through their company website is to rank among the top three listings in their field on Google. Rank position is ultimately calculated on the number of clicks received via Google searches (see Figure 5). To achieve top ranking, carefully chosen keywords and phrases relevant to potential customers' search criteria must be entered into a company's website keyword and meta tag (html) areas.

A new innovation by Google is the "+1" button on websites. This enables a registered user to click on it to recommend it automatically to their contacts through Google services (such as Gmail and Google+, the social network). The advantage of this to the website is in achieving a higher weighting on Google searches.

FIGURE 4 · *Google Search Ranking (PRO-10)*

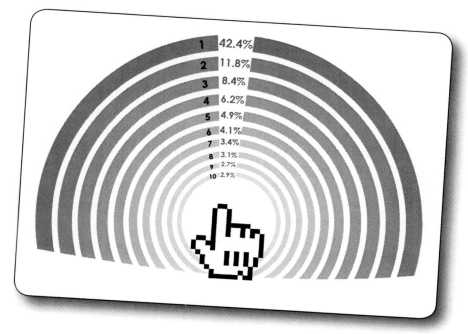

FIGURE 5 · *Percentage of Clicks by Position (www.seobook.com)*

SEO Book (www.seobook.com) estimates that about 90% of all clicks happen on the first page of search results, implying that the second page can only generate at most 10% of user traffic. Of the top three ranked sites on page one, approximately 42% of traffic goes to the website occupying position one, three times more traffic than the site which holds position two. Websites positioned in the top three gain 63% of total traffic, while the top five websites together share 74%. Therefore, benefits gained from social media will be greater if an organization can achieve a top-ranking position on Google.

Just as social media can increase a business's Google ranking, so also will rankings vary as Google's algorithm changes to reflect the needs of consumers. The extent to which a business has become an active member of communities in the global marketplace, such as Facebook and LinkedIn, will affect their company website's overall Google ranking.

1.2.2 **Global Reach**

" *Networks are open structures, able to expand without limits, integrating new nodes as long as they are able to communicate within the network, namely as long as they share the same communication codes.... A network-based social structure is a highly dynamic, open system, susceptible to innovating without threatening its balance.... Networks are appropriate instruments for a capitalist economy based on innovation, globalisation, and decentralised concentration; for work, workers and firms based on flexibility; for a culture of endless deconstruction and reconstruction; for a polity geared towards the instant processing of new values and public moods; and for a social organization aiming at the super-session of space and the annihilation of time.* **"**
(Castells, 2000, pp470–1)

Manuel Castell's *The Rise of the Network Society* sums up, very effectively, the benefits of a formal network.

An online network creates a new *space*, or *community*. This, in effect, produces instant contact with a larger audience and provides many advantages to any promotional campaign. Informal communication and social networking exists in any firm, and plays a productive role, as outlined by Waldstrøm (2003). Online networks have evolved to create more intense connections. Virtual meetings, such as those employed by Cisco, are creating new forums in which to meet people and replacing the traditional necessity of land or buildings (Hillis, 2007). As organizations desire to increase their reach and influence in the global market, allowing employees to utilize social media tools will accomplish that goal.

The question you need to ask is whether you are leading or following in your industry?

If you are leading, then you are probably already well advanced with social media. You will be looking for ways to gain serious competitive advantage through integrating it throughout your organization and with key customers. If you are a follower, then who you are following and what they are doing with social media will often determine the strategic rationale for your business.

Look for great exemplars in your industry. If you can not find any, look to other industries so that you can model them. Beware following a poor model and thinking you can tick that box, "job done." Simply opening a Facebook, Twitter, and YouTube

SocialMediaInBusiness.com

account does not do a whole lot for you. The key is whether your organization has a strategic rationale for using these tools that can be translated into business benefits. Does the leadership of your organization understand the potential of social media, how it might develop in the future, and how it can potentially impact your organization?

CASE STUDY

1.2.3 Local and Global Example – Groupon.com

Groupon is an Internet phenomenon that has achieved such success that it attracted an offer from Google to buy the business for $6 billion. Groupon turned down the offer and plans to raise more funding, with current valuations ranging from $15 to $25 billion as of June 2011.

Groupon is an example of a local business model that has gone global by using the power of the Internet and social media marketing. Groupon offers customers discounted prices and special offers redeemable at local retailers, such as restaurants, ticketed events, health and beauty shops, recreation outlets, and other goods and services providers. The power of social media gave Groupon access to global markets, allowing for the viral growth of the business.

What led to Groupon's tremendous success? Their concept requires the help of members to broker their products and services. Once an individual is signed up as a customer, they receive, via email, a new deal every day offered by local businesses. Groupon gives a clear value proposition to customers with a limiter built in, i.e. the deal is only offered for the day or for a limited number of people. If the deal does not attract a minimum number of purchases within the day, or when the deal expires, then the discount opportunity is gone. This motivates people to make snap decisions and make an effort to get the group to join the offer. It is spread virally via Facebook, Twitter, and other popular social networking channels.

AskSteve.co

Groupon buys products and services in bulk in order to provide fantastic deals to their customers. From a supplier's perspective, Groupon brings in large numbers of customers in one day, thereby boosting profits. A win-win situation is created that, as statistics have shown, motivates 97% of participating suppliers to return and work with Groupon again and again.

Groupon gets paid upfront, so it has positive cash flow by means of customer payments. After taking their cut, they pay the suppliers later, in three installments over the life of the promotion. The effectiveness of their marketing is enhanced by word-of-mouth; where customers tell their friends about a good deal via social media venues because they want to share the experience or capitalize on the deal's value.

Key insights can be gained from this example. First, Groupon has a viable business model, designed to exploit the power of social media. Second, using social media to generate viral growth through the power of recommendation is good business, since the company essentially receives free labor from their customers. Finally, viral marketing is something any business can do, regardless of size, by correctly harnessing social media. The first-mover advantage has been critical for Groupon, however, it may also be easy to copy the Groupon business model. There are currently over 200 competitors, the biggest of these being LivingSocial, bloomspot, Wahanda, and Tippr. Only time will tell.

This also shows that social media can help create new ways of doing business. This, therefore, is of interest to the strategists, business developers, and business leaders responsible for the future of the business.

By their function, social media applications build awareness of organizations, create sales leads, and create a group in which market research can take place.

 See the resource site for case studies:
www.SocialMediaInBusiness.com/Tools

1.3 **Communication**

"CONVERSATIONS
AND RELATIONSHIPS"

FIGURE 6 • *Communication*

COMMUNICATION **REFERS TO THE OPPORTUNITY** that social media provides for improving internal as well as external communications. Both aspects are amplified on social media sites. Policies must be put into place and training provided in order to give employees an understanding of what is and what is not acceptable at work, based on the culture and nature of the organization.

> **"***A social media policy has to be very clear.***"**
> See Chapter 4

1.3.1 **Internal versus External Communication**

Most businesses are complex, multi-faceted, and paradoxical in nature, creating multiple challenges for management. As a result, internal communication policies often sink to the bottom of the priority list. Broadly speaking, the purpose of internal communication is to enable the leadership of the organization to communicate with their employees in order to gain better understanding and to motivate and foster harmonious relationships, enabling employees to perform their jobs more effectively. However, internal communication flows in all directions. All the component parts of a business must communicate well with one another; top-down, bottom-up, and across many strata. The effectiveness of that communication all depends on whether the recipients are prepared to listen and whether the delivery of communication is well timed, pitched, and balanced. This is deeply influenced by the culture in the organization. Often, there are also clouded boundaries between internal employees and external contractors or clients that require skilled and careful communication strategies. Some companies eagerly embrace the social media opportunity for use within their organization, while others are more resistant.

Creating the right atmosphere in the workplace for communication is vitally important, be it to inform employees of cutbacks or pay raises, or to tell them about a new coffee machine. Effective communication will make the difference between employees reacting to a message with a positive or hostile response. The effect of internal communication determines and/or indicates the health of the entire company. Effective internal communication can inspire shared vision, loyalty, satisfaction, commitment, empowerment, and service focus.

Internal communication can be formal or informal, depending on what goal management is trying to achieve or the level of the message being delivered. It is often a department head that delivers the *official* formal message from upper management and then reinforces it through informal communication. By being the middle person, and listening to employee concerns, answering questions, and clarifying issues, managers can encourage the loyalty of employees. They also retain the confidence of upper management by shouldering communication responsibilities.

Anything that can be done to increase the effectiveness of internal communication ought to be implemented because it is so important to the organization. This could involve choosing the most appropriate channels of communication and selecting the best communicators for the task. This proper judgment and planning, coupled with a concise, coherent message, will result in members of the organization being more responsive and cohesive in both the internal and external environment.

David Bohm, a renowned physicist and innovator in the field of dialogue in organizations, suggests that conditions for communication are largely shaped by the organizational culture. Within that culture is an opportunity for organizations to embrace online social media as an informal internal communication tool. Potential benefits include improving dialogue (the sharing of assumptions and understanding) and receiving feedback that allows the company to make their products and/or services better. Social media technologies can provide a platform for organizations to create better conversations with employees in order to significantly increase effectiveness. In order for this to be achieved, however, managers must first understand the networks and how they work.

It has been acknowledged that younger staff, including recent graduates, will be more likely to be familiar with social media than their older colleagues and managers. They will have had previous experience using social media tools like Windows Live Messenger or Facebook Chat and will understandably assume that it is permissible to use these platforms in the business environment. This creates an automatic imbalance between new staff and established staff. This disparity provides an opportunity for policy-makers and middle managers to bridge the gap.

1.3.2 **Formal versus Informal Communication**

The formal organization is like the skeleton of the company, while the informal network is like the central nervous system. Crucial informal communication cuts across formal reporting procedures to facilitate better understanding of projects

AskSteve.co

and goals, and ultimately gets things done. This is a key benefit to boosting internal communications through technological means.

Much of this type of communication is spontaneous by nature. This characteristic makes it more difficult to manage, control, police, or measure. Due to its opportunistic nature and its speedy response to situations, it is also one of the most dreaded parts of a manager's job. It is rife with the possibility of negative repercussions if something is mishandled or miscommunicated.

Formal communication is based on the traditional organizational paradigm that triggers "chain of command" internal management processes. On the other hand, informal communication is based on *social relationships* between staff. Therefore, the informal communications system is:

" *...the human side of the organization, which is maintained by employees communicating among themselves and sharing information.* "

(Crampton, Hodge & Mishra, 2005)

Informal networks, by definition, have no structure. People responding to new work directives may act instantly to update their procedures, or may take days to organize themselves in line with company policy. The nature of employer-employee trust is such that managers cannot regulate how quickly employees carry out certain tasks. They are only able to measure the outcomes after the event. This is why it is entirely essential that policies be put into place in order to encourage that which is beneficial and set boundaries to contain that which is not (see section 4.5.2 on social media policies). The goal is to save time and improve efficiency. Without proper policies, the opposite could result if management has to focus on correcting improper communication activities. The manager has to be aware of the unwritten rules and the unintended consequences of any policies that are put in place.

Management can promote better informal communication by incorporating mechanisms that bring employees together. One such mechanism is the establishment of common areas in offices that visibly encourage discussion. Online social networks can be used in a similar way; only they expand on the physical space idea by virtue of their virtual nature. Communication – such as meetings – can all take place via Skype, online chat, instant messaging, and GoToMeeting-type platforms (see Chapter 3). Conversations can be carried out in real time without employees being in the same location or country. Keeping all employees updated from one social network site is simple and extremely effective. Conversations can be started, followed up on, or continued at a later date in person. This increases efficiency, well-being, and loyalty of employees by providing a place for them to be a part of something, i.e. giving them virtual *ownership,* and having their voice heard in the workplace. It can be argued that *information exchange* is the common aspect of informal communication, but it is a natural attribute of networking and not the ultimate goal.

It is rightly argued that the culture of an organization – the relationships that exist between stakeholders – provides the many variables that come together to form a picture of a company as a whole. The overall structure of a company's informal communication system must be one in which the use of technology is combined with face-to-face meetings. Online and offline networking must work in conjunction with one another, neither entirely replacing the other. Conversations that are repressed will only find unofficial outlets of expression at the water cooler, over a coffee, or through an unofficial social media source.

Social networks are also indefinably linked with corporate culture. According to Waldstrøm, 2003:

"*An organization's culture develops over time, and is slow to change, and is reinforced by the practice of people recruiting others whom they like. The informal organization, by contrast is quick to grow and transmute according to changing circumstances and the interaction of individuals within the organization.*"

Companies that simply ignore their customers on social media can also receive attention, but with negative and often costly or embarrassing results. If you claim to be transparent, then you had better stick to your word! This was the case in the Facebook–Gap logo incident. Gap, a well-known clothing retailer, revealed a new brand logo without any public warning, customer engagement, or surveying. The result of this oversight was a negative customer backlash on Gap's Facebook page that was so strong, the company had to reverse its decision to change their logo. All in all, it was a serious embarrassment that could easily have been avoided.

Both good and poor communication demonstrate the power of social media to foster a mindset to the benefit or detriment of an organization, based on the level of attention they pay to their customers. Today's consumers demand to be heard, and their joy or wrath snowballs and spreads virally on the Internet, reaching potentially millions of customers. It is critical that any business wishing to gain from the use of social media realize the importance of focusing on maintaining communications at all times in order to keep a positive edge and balance to their online campaigns.

Extreme examples of the use of social media for organizing civil uprising have been witnessed in conflicts in the Middle East, such as Egypt and Tunisia. It is clear that even repressive regimes struggle with social media, and this may be a warning for organizations hoping to control social media: at best you can listen and maybe influence it.

Ultimately, forward-thinking managers will lay out a vision for the company in which executives, management, and employees work together to achieve a common goal. Management must reassure their staff of their personal commitment to transparency, so as to attract the most dynamic new employees while retaining those that are already working for the organization. Putting in place policies for using social media at work will accomplish this.

1.3.3 An Example of Using Social Media for Reaching Out to Customers

Salesforce.com uses YouTube videos for training customers on their complex product offering. This has proven to be very successful, and according to the head of YouTube EMEA, it is believed to be worth 750 sales reps to Salesforce.com. That represents a major cost-saving and logistics advantage. The key point is, training can be leveraged using YouTube, webinars, and other online media.

1.3.4 Communication Example – Socialmedia.Cicso.com

Cisco, a global technology company, leads the way with their application of social media for a large company. You would hope they would be the leader, as this is their business. This is how they describe what they do: "Cisco is the worldwide leader in networking that transforms how people connect, communicate and collaborate." They utilize a range of social media to communicate both internally and externally with their customers, including blogs, podcasts, YouTube videos, Twitter, Facebook, Scribd, and Flickr.

Cisco describes itself as a transparent and open company, which is alien to many companies operating in fiercely competitive markets. The business environment creates something of a paradox: being open when you need to keep commercial secrets. Cisco publishes their social media policy and guidelines for their employees and makes it available on their SlideShare and Scribd channels. In the policy there is a section on how their employees are to deal with proprietary and confidential information, among other things.

Cisco clearly concentrates some resources on social media. This is not surprising given this is their business. However, Cisco provides a glimpse of the future for both large and small companies. For the manager of a small company, it may not be immediately obvious how Cisco's implementation can apply to you. The good news is that everything Cisco can do you can do, too, at a fraction of the cost, because most of the application tools they are using to communicate with the outside world are free or very low-cost. The main cost is in training, and this is a relative investment, i.e. if you are smaller, the costs are less.

How is Cisco utilizing social media? The good news is that Cisco provides a number of online resources that you can tap into. Their website (socialmedia.cisco.com) details their social media channels. At the time of writing:

AskSteve.co

- They have a directory of some 31 blogs, each aimed at different audiences, covering general information about the company, industry solutions, Cisco globally, technology, partners, corporate news, and business solutions.

- On Facebook, Cisco has 12 Facebook fan pages covering the Cisco Training Academy, support, and their products and solutions. A number of these have over 200,000 fans and foster active discussions. For example, they have a program called the SuperFan program that has over 100,000 members so far, for their most active and participating supporters (see Figure 7). A number of their communities have a Cisco community manager.

- On Twitter they have separate accounts for their products and solutions and a number of their top executives. For instance, the Cisco Chief Technology Officer, Padmasree Warrior, has over 1,390,000 followers. In turn, the 232 Twitter accounts she follows read like a technology who's who.

FIGURE 7• *A Promotion Where You Can Become a SuperFan of Cisco and Highlighted on their Facebook Page*

- On YouTube, Cisco has a very extensive YouTube channel, covering training and events, vision technology, products and services, and their partners.

- On Flickr, the photo-sharing site, they have over 1,200 photos to date (which is modest), covering their products, people, buildings, press releases, events, partners, and news.

- On SlideShare.com, for sharing presentations, Cisco is not using this channel as widely as the other social media channels (18 presentations and 7 documents), but it is a good place to find the key documents, such as the Cisco Social Media Policy, Cisco Social Media Playbook: Best Practice Sharing, and How Cisco Operationalizes Social Media for Repeated Success.

- On LinkedIn, Cisco has more than 160,000 followers on their company page. It lists 68,544 of their employees (93% of the total). Cisco also uses it to post job vacancies.

- On Apple's iTunes Store, Cisco has hundreds of free podcasts of video and audio broadcasts presenting a range of training, products, and services.

To make navigation easier from a smartphone, Cisco has a mobile-optimized version of their main website (m.cisco.com). This is a good idea, as now more and more websites are being accessed on the move via smartphones.

Cisco, in 2010, held a competition using collective intelligence (Cisco I-Prize) to come up with billion-dollar ideas. From the process, 800 ideas were submitted by 3,000 participants from 156 countries, and the winner "Rhinnovation team" won $250,000.

It is worth spending time looking at Cisco's social media, as it is transparent and available online. You will learn how they are working; they serve as a model you might be able to emulate. For a simple and fun case study, check out www.willitblend.com. It uses many of the aspects of the Cisco case but on a smaller scale.

● ● ● ● ●

1.4 **Communities**

Groups of people that share a mutual interest, passion, or idea and who congregate on specific online locations are, in general, considered to be a community. Communities can be based around an endless variety of topics: location, specific organizations, charities, hobbies, social, cultural, or religious identity, etc. They share some common characteristics based on common ideas or goals. Members usually participate in multiple conversations at the same time. In essence, they extend the offline world idea of a club, group, or service organization. From a business-to-business perspective, these communities are your market. The key to a good community is its ability to function without you at the center, i.e. self-sustaining and self-regulating.

"MANAGING CONNECTIONS"

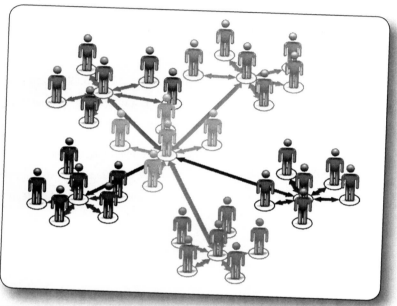

FIGURE 8 • *Communities of Interest*

Social networking platforms such as Facebook, Ning, and LinkedIn provide for a wide range of communities based around a wide range of topics, both in leisure and business. Examples of communities include book sharing, business, dating, education, expertise, fashion, lifestyle, finance, trading, forums, common goals, health, age groups (teens, students, retired), local, marketplace, shopping, mobile, music, non-profit, photo-sharing, publishing platforms, question and answer sites, social bookmarking, real estate, social networks, social search, technology, travel, and video virtual worlds. The list is only limited by the imagination and needs of community members and societal trends.

1.4.1 Relationships Mapping

While the general thrust of the statement on the right is true, one can argue that it is unduly deterministic and does not fully allow for real-life scenarios and the vagaries of politics, power, and external events. It can be argued that a medium such as online social technology would have a significant impact on this, in particular, by its rate of growth blurring any measurable pattern.

Social network analysis tries to uncover the patterns of people's interactions:

"Social structure becomes actually visible in an anthill. ...these dots do not randomly approach one another...some are usually together, some meet often, some never.... If one could get far enough away from it human life would become pure pattern."
(Brown, 1965, p785)

However, mapping employee relationships can help harness their power in your organization. Social network analysis can be used to map these relationships. To identify organizational problems, a manager can use social networks to spot common patterns such as imploded relationships, irregular communication patterns, fragile structures, and holes in networks. Knowing each employee better will lead to improved management planning and application. Companies such as Trampoline Systems are now emerging to take on this task.

FIGURE 9 • *Social Network Analysis (Cross, Nohria & Parker, 2002)*

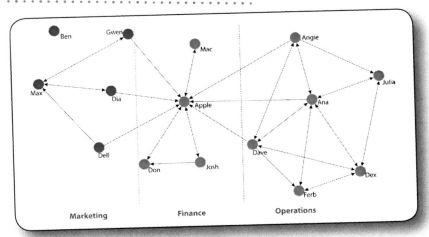

The concept of *information brokers* is described by Uzzi and Dunlop, in their 2005 research, as powerfully connected individuals whose informal communication is at the hub of all productive work efforts. Uzzi and Dunlop tried to study and codify networks of information brokers in terms of density, hubs, internal and external members, aggregate measures, and differences in perceptions. Understanding social networks is not mathematics, but a subjective exercise in context. If management can begin to perceive the patterns in employees' methods of working, they can reframe individuals' responsibilities and areas of hierarchy, and even strategically station someone's physical position to increase availability or productivity.

1.4.2 Social Capital

Social capital is a measure of what a network is worth in terms of numbers and quality, though the latter is very difficult to determine. Many companies use the Internet to expand their social capital. Connecting their business to the online world can increase their network of interactions in the hopes of increasing their reputation, popularity, customer base, etc. Morton et al (2003), stated that social capital is a quantity of active connections among trusted individuals, of mutual understanding and shared values and behavior that bind the members of networks and communities.

Mayfield (2003) proposed that social capital could grow exponentially by improving communication and ties between collaborative groups.

Online communities grow social capital via several key routes. Generally speaking, this is carried out by publishing information, linking ("friending" or "following") for communication, and forming or joining groups for collaboration.

Mayfield uses Sarnoff's, Metcalfe's, and Reed's Laws to measure the growth of social capital online:

Publishing: Sarnoff's Law says the value of a network is proportionate to the number of subscribers.

Communication: Metcalfe's Law says the value of a network is proportionate to the number of links.

Collaboration: Reed's Law says the value of a network is proportionate to the number of groups.

Though there are ways to measure the growth of network links, as they can be technically recorded or observed, quality is not so easy to track. This is because on-going trends and actions of groups can only indicate value in hindsight over the course of time. There are emerging companies that are focusing on measuring aspects of social media, e.g. www.klout.com/business, which measures an organization's online influence.

There is generally urgency for businesses to implement social media policies immediately or risk falling behind their competitors. Due to the greater access, reach, and speed of online platforms, social networking technologies are now regarded as potential company gold mines. However, online social networking also exposes organizations to external access. This is because informal communications between employees are exposed to the public eye. Naturally, this concerns managers and policy-makers who are ultimately responsible for retaining a professional corporate image for their brand.

Some companies, however, are unaware that they even have social capital and are therefore doing nothing to manage or expand it. There is a huge potential for online social networks to provide methods for increasing the number of connections between organizations and their customers. This is the social capital that the business could exploit for growth. For example, if a business draws customers primarily from the teenage demographic, it would be sensible to use the same social networks used by most teenagers.

The key principle to note is that social capital works in both positive and negative directions. Transparency in approach is essential, and changes must first be made if that is not part of an organization's current culture. If the company does not implement transparency, problems will inevitably arise during social media campaigns.

1.4.3 Six Degrees of Separation

The term *six degrees of separation*, first coined by Stanley Milgram (Watts, 2003), is often used when referring to the reach and power of a social network. This is a *small world hypothesis*, which suggests that one can reach anyone via six steps of connectivity. You are connected to your friends, who in turn are connected to their friends, who also have friends. Through this web of connectivity, within six steps we can be connected to the President of the United States, a famous celebrity, or anyone else on the planet.

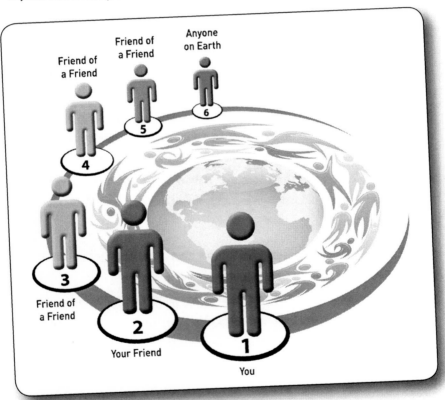

FIGURE 10 • *Six Degrees of Separation – Stanley Milgram*

Implementing this theory in the real world takes time. Making a phone call to one contact, waiting for them to send a business letter to another or attend a networking conference to find a third, can be time consuming. However, in social media circles, these links can be made in seconds. In an instant, one becomes more connected. LinkedIn, the social networking site for business professionals, is a good illustration of the six degrees of separation.

Milgram's effect, made exponentially more available through social network technologies, can literally connect a business or individual to millions of potential customers. Dunbar's Law says that 150 is the maximum number of friends or relationships a person can physically manage. However, in the online context, a person or an organization could exponentially increase their networks, with no physical limit to the number of relationships they could maintain. Posting a couple of comments daily on a social networking site could potentially connect a person or company to millions of clients over a relatively short time period.

CASE STUDY

1.4.4 Communities Example – LinkedIn.com

LinkedIn is an example of a community of business professional networkers. Launched in 2003, it was one of the main business professional networking sites available online. As of August 4, 2011, it claimed to have 115.8 million registered users (up from 50 million in 2009), in more than 200 countries. More than two million companies have LinkedIn company pages. As of June 2011, the network has executives from all 2011 Fortune 500 companies as members.

In May of 2011, LinkedIn completed an initial public offering that valued the company at over $9 billion. It had revenues of $161.4 million in the first nine months of 2010, and a profit of $1.85 million. The main source of LinkedIn revenues came from job listings (41%), advertising (32%), and premium subscriptions (27%).

LinkedIn uses the Stanley Milgram *six degrees of separation* principle and even shows users of the site how many degrees away from themselves are the people they want to connect with. For example, if a person wanted an introduction to President Barack Obama, and he was just two steps away via community contacts, making a request to the closest business connection could result in a direct connection being made to the president through only one step. The person who is two degrees (contacts) away could ask the mutually trusted contact to make the introduction.

LinkedIn can be used in a number of ways. Posting a professional profile of key company figureheads, complete with online resumes and pictures, builds recognition. It also certainly helps where there is more than one person with the same name. For instance, a search for the name Steve Nicholls revealed 194 people on LinkedIn as of January 2011. Establishing a detailed profile is the best way of managing an online persona and allows an individual or organization to control what they want people to see about themselves or their company.

LinkedIn also provides the means for members of the community to find jobs and business opportunities. Employers list jobs, and job seekers can look for someone in their network to give them an introduction. Job postings are categorized by keyword, company, industry, location, country, postal code, or company size. Users can then access companies that are hiring by viewing these listings. It is also a place to connect or reconnect with high school or university alumni and colleagues from previous organizations.

LinkedIn also has a company search feature that enables users to search for a specific organization and locate specific statistics or descriptions of a company. Members can view a company profile, find related companies, locate profiles of company employees, view new hires, and gain access to information on recent promotional campaigns and any organizational changes that may have recently occurred. The benefits of accessing this type of information are profound if an individual or organization is looking to do business with a certain company.

SocialMediaInBusiness.com

Another feature of LinkedIn is the Groups area, where members can further increase the number of connections they seek to make. Individuals or companies can create a group, join a group, and look at the groups to which others belong. There is also a feature that recommends groups that a user might like. These recommendations are a reflection of the site's database, which categorizes data based on member choices. Users can then view, follow, and participate in discussions that are started within a group. Key group categories to be considered for good networking are alumni groups, corporate groups, conference groups, networking groups, non-profit groups, professional groups, and other groups related to one's business.

LinkedIn Answers is an area on the site where individuals or company representatives can raise a question and people in the community can answer. Answers receive scores and rankings based on member feedback. This is an avenue for people to elevate their profile and present themselves as a thinker, leader, and expert based on feedback they provide on specific topics related to their business.

Other examples of applications integrated into the LinkedIn community site are SlideShare and TripIt. SlideShare is a feature that allows the sharing of presentations. TripIt allows members to share their travel destinations and propose meeting up with people in their network who live in the destination area. A mobile version of the site is also available for use on mobile devices when members are on the move. More applications continue to be added as the community grows and evolves.

Much can be learned from the LinkedIn example. It demonstrates the mutually beneficial nature of a self-sustaining online community and serves as a great example of what a good online community could do for its members.

• • • • •

AskSteve.co

1.5 **Collective Intelligence**

"ACCESSING IDEAS"

FIGURE 11 • *Collective Intelligence*

THE FORWARD-THINKING MANAGER must assess the business to determine if it is fully accessing the pool of expertise available within the organization. It is equally important to tap into the supply chain, customers, and the online community in order to gain access to the full spectrum of resources available for maximizing productivity. By gathering multiple viewpoints, businesses secure access to collective intelligence. This helps to attain the goal of enhancing the quality of ideas and improving decision making within the organization. Businesses that do not tap into this resource afforded by social media outlets are missing a valuable opportunity to gain insights on a wide range of topics.

Tim O'Reilly (2005) describes collective intelligence as a web community that functions as a kind of global brain, and claims that it reflects conscious thought and attention. It is also known as *crowd smarts*, tapping into a new "gene pool" of thinkers who can work independently on a common issue. As the community gains critical mass and attracts more people, the quality of the content improves and becomes more relevant to the users. Crowd smarts can improve decision making by allowing access to diverse views and corresponding feedback in quick succession.

Although collective intelligence operates in normal (offline) internal communication, its value is greatly enhanced by online social networks because of their inherent advantages, like speed and breadth of audience. By utilizing employees' familiarity with current social network sites, businesses can leapfrog any initial concerns and target the best social media choices in their industry.

Social networks boost the crowd smarts approach, as James Surowiecki's theory (2005) suggests:

"The paradox of the wisdom of the crowd is that the best decision comes from lots of independent decisions."

The quotation above suggests that a group of independent experts are more likely to come up with a better result than a team of experts working together as one. This is achieved due to several constructs existing in the online social community: diversity of opinions, independence from political or cultural interference, capacity to draw on specialist and local knowledge, and ability to gather individual ideas into a collective decision.

Hoegg et al (2006) and O'Reilly (2005) have similar interpretations that provide valuable insight. They agree that in order to maximize the benefits of collective intelligence, a community must be self-regulatory. The community must also, however, have clearly defined boundaries within which relevant thoughts can be shared. This is the only form of moderation or regulation that needs to take place. Furthermore, there remains an issue in regards to ensuring accuracy of the information (Kolbitsch and Maurer, 2006). A high level of trust is required when accessing and using any information found on online forums. Users must therefore ensure that they are posting factual information.

On the other hand, group bias can result in the absence of sufficient diversity. Lack of independent insight can create *groupthink*, which occurs when the community

AskSteve.co

members are influenced by the other members. *Groupthink* is defined by Janis (1982) as the behavior of people thinking as a cohesive group, in which members' strivings for unanimity override their motivation to realistically appraise alternative courses of action.

According to Surowiecki (2005), the most important lesson lies in not relying on the wisdom of one or two experts or leaders before making difficult decisions. Online social networks have great potential benefits in terms of providing diversity, abundant information, and a forum to voice different opinions. However, the issues of light-touch regulation and trust are still relevant. Although there is plenty of literature on organizational trust, in general, there is little on trust that specifically relates to online social networks. Interestingly, many organizations still operate on a hierarchical basis and principally rely on the opinions of one or two experts or leaders before making difficult decisions.

Collective intelligence can take the form of a "recommendation system" that is built into a website, such as that which is utilized by Amazon (www.amazon.com). As customers browse the site, Amazon provides them with recommendations based on their previous browsing and buying history, and compares their selections to other customers' popular choices of similar products. In effect, they are sharing the collective intelligence of the greater buying community to assist customers in choosing products. This in turn has the potential of increasing sales if a shopper becomes interested in another product based on the site's recommendations.

Additionally, recommendation and buyer feedback components have similar effects on buying behavior. For example, TripAdvisor (www.tripadvisor.com) allows members to post comments on their trip experiences. Current travelers can read reviews and make decisions based on the ratings of services shared by the other users. Since people don't want to stay at hotels with poor ratings, the buyer feedback feature becomes an effective tool in keeping discriminating customers on their site and using their services. Amazon.com has a similar feedback function, where customers can rate books and other products they have purchased. Consumers can gather much insight from this kind of collective intelligence.

Wikis are great examples of collective intelligence. A wiki is a website that allows users to create and edit, with a simple text editor, any number of interlinked web pages via a web browser. Wikis are often used to create collaborative works. Examples include corporate intranets, community-based websites, and knowledge data systems. Some wikis can give varying degrees of access to different types of users. For example, editing rights may permit the general public to add, delete, or change material, but only administrators or authors generally would have admin level of access. Other rules may apply, as unique wiki website functions differ.

Wikipedia (www.wikipedia.org) is the most well-known wiki online today. It features a free online encyclopedic database of information on literally millions of topics. Users can add their own entries, as long as they are informative and as factual as possible. Ranking number seven in the most-visited websites, hundreds of millions of people regularly use the site as a quick reference guide and also to disseminate more information into the collective public community.

Recently WikiLeaks (www.wikileaks.org), a whistle blower site, gained notoriety for leaking 250,000 U.S. diplomatic cables into the public sector. WikiLeaks.org is an international non-profit wiki that publishes private, secret, and classified information from anonymous news sources and media leaks. Its database contained over a million documents within a year of its launch. The site began as a user-editable wiki, but no longer accepts user comments or edits. (See page 112 for further examples of wikis, including DIY wiki platforms.)

Although crowdsourcing is very similar to collective intelligence, it is not the same thing. Crowdsourcing is the act of outsourcing tasks, normally assigned to an employee or contractor, to an undefined, large number of knowledgeable people, or "crowd." Crowdsourcing can be classified in this section as collective intelligence, but it is also considered to be collaboration since a large group of individuals is assigned a single task. Contributions are generally invited via forums and are answered on a voluntary basis. Yahoo! Answers has collated a vast database of information by such means. More such applications and services are being created as the marketplace evolves.

AskSteve.co

A prime example of utilizing collective intelligence "on the move" (24 hours a day in real time) is Dell Corporation through their Corporation's Listening Command Center, which actively monitors social media channels in 11 different languages for references to Dell and the competition. The stated purpose is active intervention in the areas of customer service issues, new product ideas, ratings and reviews, brand reputation, and marketing, to name a few. Examples are acknowledging feedback (people want to know they have been heard) and spotting challenges early, before they become bigger.

CASE STUDY

1.5.1 Collective Intelligence Example – My Starbucks Idea

Starbucks is a good example of a company that is both local and global. Most of us have a Starbucks coffee shop nearby. Starbucks uses social media very effectively. They have over 24 million "friends" on their Facebook fan page. They use collective intelligence to do market research on their products and services, as demonstrated by the consumer polls that can be found on their fan page (www.facebook.com/Starbucks). They also have a separate website, MyStarbucksIdea (mystarbucksidea.force.com), where Starbucks taps into their customer base for:

- **Product ideas:** Drinks, food, merchandise, music, store charge card, new technology, and other product-related ideas.

- **Customer experience ideas:** Ordering, payment, order pick-up, atmosphere, locations, and other experience-related ideas.

- **Involvement ideas:** Building community, social responsibility, and miscellaneous involvement ideas.

The Starbucks example demonstrates a company that is listening to their customers and earning huge payoffs in return. The special relationship they have created through social media sites has increased customer loyalty. Tapping into the collective intelligence of their customer base has also facilitated improvements to their local outlets, all freely offered by their "fans."

SocialMediaInBusiness.com

Starbucks is obviously a very large company and can launch large campaigns to increase customer loyalty. The amazing thing about social media, however, is that the same tools are available to even the smallest companies for free. To the extent that a small business uses the tools available on sites like Facebook, they can, though perhaps on a smaller scale, access customer ideas and insights, using collective intelligence to increase their social capital.

Other businesses are exploring ideas in a systematic way, similar to the Starbucks model, through a variety of methods using collective intelligence. Some organizations, such as NASA, The Economist, and Netflix, have run competitions to gather data. They offer cash incentives to encourage participation and use online resources, such as InnoCentive (www.innocentive.com), to facilitate the process.

• • • • •

1.6 **Collaboration**

"EFFECTIVE WORKING PARTNERSHIPS"

FIGURE 12 • *Collaboration Model for Competitive Advantage*

THERE ARE MANY FORMS of collaboration. The five main types that we find predominantly in social media circles are:

● Conversation: email, instant messaging, e.g. Facebook

● Coordination: project management, e.g. Wrike.com

● Cooperation: crowdsourcing, e.g. Yahoo! Answers

● Co-creation: wiki websites, e.g. Wikipedia

● Collective Action: petitions, fundraising, e.g. Petitionbuzz.com

The general term *collaboration* (co-laboring) is a label given to describe participation among groups of individuals: employees, teams, departments, and also bilateral groups such as business/customers, business/suppliers, and business/stakeholders.

Collaboration also needs to be considered as an adjunct to communication (see section 1.3). Communication and collaboration within an organizational structure, whether in the office or online, is greatly enhanced or degraded by the degree of trust and consistency of work habits.

Collaboration and collective intelligence go hand in hand. Online social media technologies enable users to engage in activities that enhance both personal and business aspects of their lives. Online networking allows for the rapid creation of a new, easy to manage *forum*, or *community*, in which all levels of collaboration can take place. Unlike traditional time-consuming meetings in a physical office space, online groups react with almost instant speed, allowing the use of the virtual meeting space to build new connections and solve relevant problems and challenges rapidly and with greater (collective) participant input.

According to Tapscott and Williams (2005), collaboration occurs in a cascading pattern, suggesting that organizations can encourage informal interactions to facilitate idea expansion. Social media enables organizations to collaborate at different levels; among employees, firms, and stakeholders across departments. Taking advantage of media like mobile devices (iPhone, iPad, Android, BlackBerry devices, and the like), also demonstrates a fundamental benefit of new web technologies. Technology is

SocialMediaInBusiness.com

now so pervasive that it is commonly found in everyday modern culture. Increasingly sophisticated devices are regularly added to the market. Mobile-smart devices, like the iPhone, iPad, Samsung tablet, etc., as well as home entertainment units, such as Wii and Xbox, are now interconnected with the Internet to such a degree that people anywhere in the world can communicate and even play games with one another.

Organizations' assets can be tagged and managed using RFID (radio-frequency identification). Technological advances allow today's day-to-day functions to be remotely controlled and monitored. If a person loses their iPhone, an Internet application can be activated to find it. Networks of interconnected devices can now effectively collaborate with each other to the benefit of their users. The level of technological sophistication continues to increase with each new generation of products. The world is now permeated with inter-connected equipment that has implications for both organizations and the home.

1.6.1 **Internal Collaboration**

Teamwork is the essence of sharing and collaborating. Technology allows for knowledge to be easily pooled, stored, and repeatedly referenced. Online collaboration tools make it really easy to share information and facilitate project advancement efficiently and effectively.

Social networking tools empower users to collaborate while talking face-to-face, regardless of their location. People on opposite sides of the world can now use video technology to communicate with one another as if they were seated at the other side of the table. This sort of collaboration is becoming more and more common as technology advances. Video conferencing is especially useful when one party is in a remote location or when it is otherwise geographically impossible for people to meet in person.

It is very common for organizations to have projects in progress where effective communication and collaboration are necessary. Document sharing helps teams coordinate individual efforts and make progress towards project completion.

Information control has always been a key issue in project management, as a large amount of data must be shared among team members. Since many versions of documentation can exist among those involved in the project, online applications increase accuracy; an update can be sent instantly, and users can replace an older version with the new at the push of a button.

Working across silos has traditionally posed many problems for organizations. One of the major issues encountered is that each department has to "reinvent the wheel." Due to lack of technological connectivity, many companies have lagged behind, still using out-dated legacy IT systems. Also, an organization's silo may vary in regard to culture, politics, and departmental procedures. This variation prevents their various working environments from being conducive to the sharing of data and ideas.

Effective collaboration across silos is now made possible by advances in broadband networks. Internet connectivity and social media applications enable team members in remote locations to work together. Different departments can now share common project information, create libraries of data that can be accessed from anywhere, and create remote training programs. Wiki applications in particular work well in these types of settings.

1.6.2 **External Collaboration**

Communication between an organization and others who wish to collaborate (such as customers or suppliers) can present difficulties. Since IT, security, and other procedures are different for each entity, issues can arise. The need for effective collaboration is often high when there are benefits for both sides of the partnership, but only if they can work together efficiently and productively to meet goals. Email is no longer the most effective way to share information, as individuals are regularly swamped with both personal and business emails that are not directly relevant to the projects in which they are involved. When working with contracted staff, consultants, or other outsourced workers, the boundaries of the organization (internal vs. external) can often be blurred. Social media creates the ability to

SocialMediaInBusiness.com

improve communication with external partners and services, so that ultimately goals can be met and operational costs kept down. Using an extranet application with a client is an example of how social media can make and enhance collaboration in the workplace.

Organizations willing to share different types of information can effectively collaborate with communities that are in some way related to them. As previously noted, Facebook, Google, WordPress blogs, and YouTube are open platforms that enable sharing on an unprecedented scale. A potential customer might comment on an organization's Facebook page, may joke about its latest promotion, or ask a question about a new product. Businesses may introduce or highlight other parts of their organization in order to meet the needs of clients and customers or help solve a problem. This can result in new clients, increased customer respect and support, and build-up of company reputation.

CASE STUDY

1.6.3 Collaboration Example – Accenture

Accenture is a global management consulting, technology services, and outsourcing company. It is the largest consulting firm in the world, with over 200,000 employees in 120 countries spanning the globe. Accenture's "borderless workplace" is one of the best examples of collaboration in the world today. Accenture is a Fortune Global 500 company, and clients include many Fortune Global 100 and 500 companies.

Since they are a consulting company, people are their key asset. Accenture's people wanted better access to each other's goods and services, as well as to the vast knowledge base that could be available to them through sharing. Being a global company with people spread all over the world, face-to-face collaboration would be expensive and generally impractical. Since younger staff members were already interacting on Facebook, LinkedIn, Twitter, and YouTube, as well as using wikis, Accenture capitalized on social media in order to meet

AskSteve.co

the requests of their worldwide community. They created Accenture People, a closed communication network modeled on Facebook, LinkedIn, and Bebo. Over 100,000 employees created profiles, and one-third of the staff is now using Accenture-related social media every month.

Accenture created the Accenture Knowledge Exchange, enabling employees to share proposals, exchange work plans for projects, and participate in a question and answer forum. Besides this interactive form of sharing knowledge, Accenture created the Accenture Encyclopedia, a white-labeled version of Wikipedia. This database provides additional resources for individuals belonging to their global community who are seeking more information on any given topic.

To further complement their repertoire of collaborative venues, they created Accenture Media Exchange, a video-sharing application similar in function to YouTube. It also boasts a video-conferencing feature, with webcams providing 360 degree views of conference rooms in a number of key Accenture locations across the globe. This enables their people to share knowledge, provide training, and collaborate on projects from nearly anywhere in the world.

Accenture continues to experiment and roll out new tools based on the major social media sites for both internal and external use. The main issues they are concerned with are not technology. They are interested in changing working practices and encouraging employees to work in new ways. Training is very important in achieving these goals. They are also using these tools to collaborate with their customers using micro sites for virtual team-working and for sharing information.

As discussed in the Starbucks collective intelligence example, businesses do not have to be global consulting firms to exploit social media for collaboration in the same fashion as Accenture. Tools such as Facebook are free, and an expensive IT department does not need to be set up in order to access it. Just a few short years ago, this type of global reach was impossible without an enormous budget and staff to keep equipment running smoothly. Today, social media tools are either free or customized specifically for a firm for a very low, pay-as-you-go fee. Most applications can be "cloned" or "white-labeled" and branded specifically for a company's work environment.

Additionally, smaller companies sometimes have an advantage over large entities when it comes to utilizing available applications. Online services and virtual products can be purchased at very reasonable costs, and many are free for smaller accounts. For instance, Dropbox (www.dropbox.com) is a file sharing and storage service that provides 2 GB of space for free and charges reasonable fees for firms needing more space. This type of venue is ideal for ad hoc sharing of large files, making collaboration easier and much quicker. Smaller, more virtually agile firms have an advantage in that they can experiment and try new services as they emerge on the market. A large firm requires more planning and may have more red tape, as well as IT constraints to work through, before using applications effectively.

This example demonstrates that there are more tools for collaboration available today than ever before, making working with other individuals, groups, or communities extremely easy and potentially profitable. The difficulty is not in finding applications, but in deciding which applications will best serve a company's needs. Understanding the function of specific applications and implementing them effectively will be presented in greater detail in later chapters.

● ● ● ● ●

AskSteve.co

1.7
Take Away Points

● ● ● ● ●

- The ultimate goal available to any business thinking of using social media is the cherished goal of increased market visibility.

- There are exciting possibilities available to businesses today by accessing a myriad of social media tools and platforms to enhance their growth.

- In order to take advantage of these opportunities, managers must implement a comprehensive social media strategy that complies with organizational policies, as well as sales and marketing plans. This will allow the company to reap the greatest benefits available while avoiding the pitfalls that exist when using social media platforms.

- Despite the opportunities readily available to be exploited for company gain, social media is not a panacea – the rules of business still apply. Managers must be aware that the benefits derived from using social media are profoundly influenced by the interior culture, power structure, and politics of their organization.

- There are four primary opportunities to be considered:

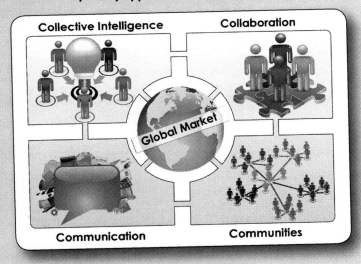

CHAPTER 2

• • • • •

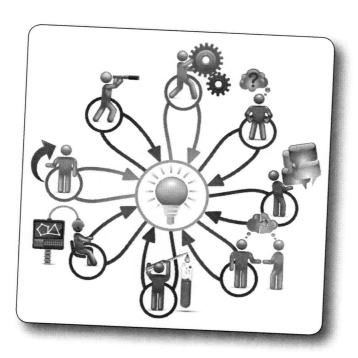

Social Media Development

IN THE PREVIOUS CHAPTER the four major opportunities offered by social media were discussed. This chapter presents the background to social media and how it evolved into these four opportunities. It analyzes the seismic shift that is taking place in the Internet, which is going through a major evolution and will continue to do so for the foreseeable future, to Web 2.0 and beyond.

Not only is the Internet changing but also the way we are accessing it is changing. The increasing popularity of Internet-enabled mobile devices, and the fact that we can now access the Internet on our television screens, have dramatically changed our experience of the Internet.

The future and health of any business depends on its growth. Finding innovative ways of growing a business can secure its competitive advantage in its industry. Such measures require unconventional approaches. Fierce competition can be expected among companies who are determined to enhance their business positions by exploiting all available tools. For those resolute enough to always be one step ahead of their competitors, keeping up with technologies is not an option; it is a precondition to success.

● ● ● ● ●

2.1 **Evolution of the Internet**

SOCIAL MEDIA CAN BE SEEN as one of the results of a broader change in the Internet. This is a fundamental shift that is best summed up as a move away from information gathering to an emphasis on user participation. Any significant change in the Internet as a whole requires some degree of adjustment to the way companies interact with it.

The latest version of the Internet, known as "Web 2.0" or "Web Squared," as coined by Tim O'Reilly, has a whole host of online applications that will increasingly impact organizations. This topic will be taken up in Chapter 4. The Meme Map below, created by Tim O'Reilly (2005), is widely cited for its portrayal of the core principles of Web 2.0 applications.

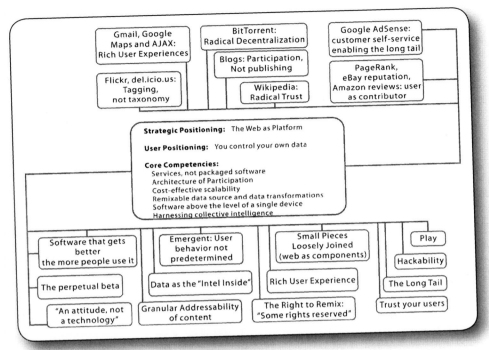

FIGURE 13 · *Web 2.0 Meme Map*

In the past, a computer terminal linked to the Internet was a stand-alone component in an office, used for fact checking, research, or data storage. Now, with the advent of social networks, a PC terminal is a window, a door, a post box, a coffee room, or an entertainment portal. It is, in fact, a host of access points to your business. It has moved out of the corner and has become the hub of many offices. Constant connection to the Internet enables you to keep abreast with developments across the global arena in real time. Similarly, external parties can see, hear, and, potentially, invest in you.

Social media enables you to participate in multiple quantum worlds around you. While sitting at your desk or on the move with a mobile device, you can also be interacting in many different arenas online. In addition, user participation enables you to combine work and family life, business and pleasure, more efficiently, resulting in the best or worst of both worlds. Always being available leads to the blurring of the boundary between work life and personal life.

The Internet has evolved into **"*a giant programmable computer that anyone can use.*"** (Don Tapscott, author of *Wikinomics*)

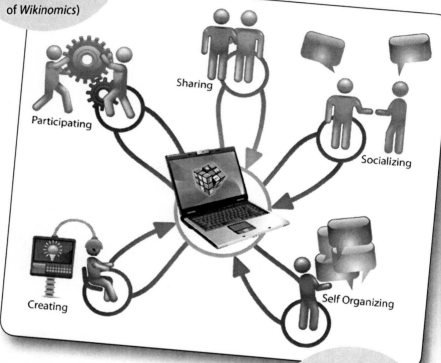

FIGURE 14 • *Internet, the Giant Computer*

"*...The new Web is principally about participation rather than about passively receiving information.*" (Tapscott and Williams, 2005, p56)

SocialMediaInBusiness.com

2.2 **The Changing Social Media Landscape**

FIGURE 15 AND FIGURE 16 (see pages 70, 71) published by XKCD.com, illustrate how the social media landscape changed between 2007 and 2010. The most striking thing in the three years since the first map was drawn is the meteoric rise of Facebook, Twitter, and Skype, as well as QQ in China. Within Facebook, games like Farmville and Happy Farm have also become wildly popular. It is interesting to note the decline in the popularity of MySpace, AOL, and Windows Live. Given these startling developments in social media over the past three years, one might wonder what is going to happen in the next three years and, more importantly, how to keep on top of such a dynamic picture. The cyber world is ever-changing and the landscape is still evolving.

Global Ranking Alexa.com (as at 31 December 2007)	Global Ranking Alexa.com (as at 31 December 2010)	Site	Function	Launched
1	(4)	Yahoo!	Marketplace (portal)	Mar 1998
2	(1)	Google	Search Engine	Sept 1998
3	(8)	Windows Live	Search Engine	Dec 2005
4	(3)	YouTube	Sharing videos	Dec 2005
5	(11)	MSN	Marketplace (portal)	Aug 2005
6	(-)	MySpace	Social Network	Jan 2004
7	(2)	Facebook	Social Network	Feb 2005
8	(7)	Wikipedia	Encyclopedia	Jan 2001
9	(-)	Hi5	Social Network	Jun 2003
10	(-)	Orkut	Social Network	Jan 2004
-	5	Blogger	Blog	Aug 1999
-	6	Baidu	Search Engine – China	Jan 2000
-	9	Twitter	Microblog	July 2006
-	10	QQ	Search Engine – China	Nov 1998

Source: www.alexa.com/topsites

TABLE 1 · *Social Media Sites with Most Traffic, 2007–2010*

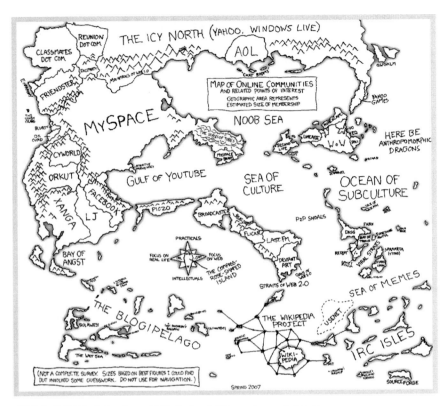

FIGURE 15 • *Social Media Landscape 2007 – by Randall Munroe (www.xkcd.com)*

The changing social media landscape is presented another way in Table 1. Alexa.com uses traffic ranking to gauge the dominance of social media's major players.

The changing dominance of social media players we observed previously on the maps is again apparent in the above table. Within just a few years Google, YouTube, Facebook, and Wikipedia have risen through the ranks, with Facebook making the steepest rise, from the 8th to the 2nd highest position in Alexa traffic ranking.

The popularity of the previously dominant social media websites such as Yahoo!, Windows Live, and MSN seem to have declined over the three years. Hi5, Orkut, and MySpace appear to have dropped out of the top ten altogether in December 2010. Indeed, Hi5, Orkut, and MySpace have plunged to the 388th, 97th, and 85th

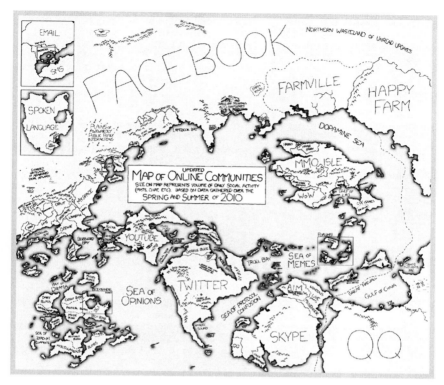

FIGURE 16 • *Social Media Landscape 2010 – by Randall Munroe (www.xkcd.com)*
(See www.SocialMediaInBusiness.com/538 for the full image)

position, respectively, as of July 2011. In contrast, websites such as Blogger, Baidu, Twitter, and QQ have risen up to the 5th, 6th, 9th, and 10th of the traffic rank to join the prestigious top ten most popular websites.

It is interesting to note that the top ten most successful websites of 2010 were launched in the late 1990s to early 2000s. It took some of them over 10 years to rise through the traffic rank, while others like Facebook and YouTube took half as long to reach the top three positions. It appears to be equally fast for some websites to lose their positions in the top ten traffic ranking.

Given the volatile nature of the social media landscape, it is hard to predict what would happen in three years. The most popular websites of today may be overtaken by entirely new players in a few years' time. However, by keeping a keen eye on key players and where, generally, social media technology is heading, we could perhaps prepare ourselves for any emerging popular websites. After all, the important thing is to be accessible via the most popular websites our customers are using.

The key point for a manager to note is that the popularity of social media sites changes over time. It is therefore important to have an understanding of the social media landscape and to stay on top of its evolution.

● ● ● ● ●

2.3 **Rise of Mobility**

DESPITE THE RELATIVELY SHORT TIME social media has been on the market, its impact on our society is undeniable. It is, therefore, worthwhile for managers to be on the continuous lookout for new technology; to think of ways to use it to benefit their organization. For example, some new technological advances that are currently becoming more popular are augmented reality and QR codes.

2010 has been a prosperous year for the smartphone and tablet computer, led by Apple. The appeal and functionality of the major smartphone platforms, such as iPhone, Google Android, RIM BlackBerry, and Nokia with Microsoft Windows, continues to draw many customers. As reported by International Data Corporation (IDC), the number of smartphones sold in 2010 totaled 302.6 million (IDC, 2011). Smartphones accounted for 297 million (18%) of the 1.6 billion mobile phones sold in 2010, according to Gartner (2011).

Tablet PCs are another rising trend when it comes to mobile computing. Again according to IDC, an estimated 17 million tablets (Apple and others) were shipped globally in 2010. That number is expected to increase drastically in 2011, with an estimated 44.6 million tablets shipped (Reisinger, 2011).

In 2011, according to Gartner, 17.7 billion apps generated $15 billion spent on mobile apps. Their prediction is for 21.6 billion apps to be sold in 2013 for a total of $29.5 billion. This highlights the scale of growth in a very new market.

FIGURE 17 ● *Mobility: Smartphones and Tablet Computers*

This gives birth to a whole new class of computing on the move and opens up a whole new area of opportunity that an organization can tap. Below are some examples:

● **Healthcare** – instead of traditional paper charts, doctors and nurses can use iPads and other mobile devices when consulting with their patients. They can easily access all relevant patient information at the click of a button.

● **Boutiques** – Burberry staff have been using iPads to help in-store customers with their purchases. A custom application also allows their customers to browse fashion shows and purchase an item from the collection while on the go.

AskSteve.co

- **Sales People** – During tradeshows and other off-site sales activities, iPads and other mobile computing devices allow instant access to product information, pricing, order information, and other customer resources. Mercedes-Benz is known to use iPads in the sales process. These mobile devices allow sales representatives to record key customer information from anywhere on the site, for instance, while standing next to the car being sold. Andreas Hinrichs, VP of Marketing for Mercedes-Benz Financial, said, "The iPad will provide a competitive advantage to our dealers by increasing their service levels through a more flexible financing process" (Businessinsider.com, 2010).

- **Restaurants** – In this environment customers can use iPads or tablets to select from onscreen menus and send their orders directly to the bar and kitchen. This has a number of advantages, such as the ability for the restaurant to provide the menu in different languages or to provide additional information about the menu and the restaurant.

- **Hotels and Resorts** – Founder and CEO of Incentient, Pat Martucci states, "Consumers expect technologies in their lives" (Businessinsider.com, 2010). Incentient creates a platform to enable efficient communication between hotel guests and different hotel departments like room service and housekeeping.

When it comes to business, iPads and other tablets are key tools that can be used to open up endless possibilities of growing a business, increasing efficiency, and improving customer service.

2.3.1 Augmented Reality on Mobiles

Augmented reality can be described as the use of technology to overlay computer-generated content on top of live images captured through cameras. Although still in its infancy, augmented reality technology is becoming more accessible and affordable enough for use on tablets and smartphones.

For example, location-based services use augmented reality technology to allow mobile users to gather crowdsourced data about a specific location and their surroundings. Real-time images are captured through your camera and are then superimposed with media from Flickr or Wikipedia through the use of augmented reality technology. This can be exploited by businesses to announce promotions to increasingly mobile audiences. Business establishments can also advertise a promotion or distribute coupons using augmented reality technology.

There are many examples of augmented reality applications that can be downloaded free to your smartphone:

* Layar overlays different information about your location, such as related pictures from Flickr or the locations of nearby cinemas, museums, or events currently taking place. According to their website, this application has over one thousand layers available.

* Wikitude is a travel guide integrated with relevant information from the online encyclopedia, Wikipedia. This application allows users to access all the available Wikipedia articles about the location in which they are currently situated.

Augmented reality technology has a powerful potential for future applications in terms of enhancing the user's mobile experience and improving their lifestyle and business. The key is to experiment with emerging tools for your business and discover where you can integrate them into your business processes.

2.3.2 **Rise of QR Codes and Microsoft Tags**

FIGURE 18 •

Scan QR Code or Microsoft Tag for www.smqrcode.com
• • • • • • • • • •

QR codes (and Microsoft Tags) are similar to barcodes that are commonly used for tracking of inventory and the price of products at the point of purchase. However, QR codes hold more information than traditional barcodes in that they have the ability to encode thousands of pieces of alphanumeric information in a smaller space. A compatible software application (app) on the user's mobile device reads the code and triggers specific actions, such as downloading a file or launching a website. When combined with a smartphone application, QR codes can be a very potent business tool. ConnectMeQR.com is an example of an application utilizing QR code technology to forward the user to a mobile site (see examples in Figure 18, both of which will take you to www.SMQRcode.com when scanned with the appropriate scanner app on your mobile phone).

QR codes can be scanned or read using most Android, BlackBerry, iPhone, and specific camera-enabled smartphone devices. The software needed to read the code can be downloaded for free.

QR codes are easy to generate and allow organizations to link to a wealth of information that can then be accessed by anyone with a mobile device. Linking the QR code to a specific location on your web site offers a lot of possibilities, for example:

● A buyer can get product information, such as installation instructions.

● There is access to unlimited sharing of data.

● Likify.net has a free service that enables you to create a QR code to link a mobile device directly to the 'like' button of a Facebook fan page. This enables the user to automatically join that fan page.

● Organizations can link codes to a "call to action" landing page featuring special offers.

QR codes/Microsoft Tags will most likely only catch on when readers become a standard feature on mobile devices. This emerging technology is one to watch.

● ● ● ● ●

2.4 **Rise of Cloud Computing**

IF YOU OWN AN EMAIL ACCOUNT with an Internet-based provider like Hotmail or Gmail, then you've already had some experience with cloud computing. Cloud computing greatly increases existing IT capabilities without the need to license new software, incur additional training expenses, or invest in new communications and infrastructures. It allows organizations to access any required files and applications using the Internet via any device, making sharing media much easier. When you have content that you want to access on multiple devices and with multiple people, then having a central storage space for your files is a major benefit. Apple has recently launched their service called iCloud that rivals services from Amazon and Google.

According to IDC, customers are projected to spend $42 billion on cloud computing by 2012 (Gens, 2008). It has been predicted by Coda Research Consultancy that by 2015, cloud computing will capture 17% of all IT expenditure globally. This is expected to bring worldwide revenues up from $46 billion in 2008 to $180 billion.

It includes pay-per-use service for basic features or subscription-based service for more advanced applications.

FIGURE 19 • *Rise of Cloud Computing*

The main benefit of cloud computing is that it works on a "pay as you go" basis. Software as a service (SaaS) minimizes the cost of maintaining necessary business applications, as opposed to using conventional hosting services. It also offers customers software licensing or server use at no cost. Example uses are:

● **Email** – Access to email is vital to every business, as it has become a standard means of communication. Maintaining or keeping track of passwords and users, along with sharing email account information, is cumbersome. Thanks to evolving information technology, most cloud email services today offer more than just the computer-based alternatives – for free. Examples are: MailChimp for newsletters and Gmail by Google.

● **Office Applications and Project Management** – Cloud computing makes project management easy, inexpensive, and efficient. It provides a myriad of project management programs to run, manage, and keep track of time and tasks. Basecamp and Zoho Projects are just two examples of project management programs. Organizations can also access different office applications, such as Microsoft Office Live, Evernote, and Google Docs in the "cloud" to trim down organizational expenses.

● **Backups, Shared Storage, and Communication** – It is critical for the business to back up documents and files. Cloud computing ensures the safety of essential data by running online automated backup programs, such as Crashplan, Carbonite, and AVG LiveKive. Box.net and Dropbox are applications that offer well-organized and secure sharing of files among colleagues. Cloud computing is also a key contributor in achieving less costly but reliable communications through Voice over Internet Protocol (VoIP). Examples of VoIP services are Skype and MyNetFone.

The growing popularity of cloud computing platforms, however, is rife with security issues. Users are typically concerned about transparency, reliability, security, and the interoperability of applications and software across cloud services. IT suppliers must therefore work together with business organizations to establish a relationship of trust when using cloud services.

Regardless of these issues, cloud computing is a highly regarded asset to improve business operations while reducing expenses.

• • • • •

2.5 Rise of Internet on our Television Screens

GIVEN THE TREND FOR THE SALES of large flat screen television sets in homes and businesses and the widespread use of broadband, it has become possible to access a big screen view of the Internet via a television set. This allows for a completely different experience than accessing a website from your smartphone screen. Modern flat screen TVs enable the user to wirelessly send content from their computer or mobile device to the large screen.

It is now possible for users to stream content on demand – from services such as Ustream.tv, BBC iPlayer, and YouTube – as well as to have Skype calls and Twitter feeds on their TV. From a business perspective, every organization is now in the broadcasting business. Where is this going in the future, especially when combined with cloud computing and mobility? The future of broadcasting and media sharing shall be very interesting, as it will enable a whole range of different innovations that have not yet been invented.

There are concerns about the Internet's ability to handle the traffic as this service grows. The ability of the Internet to adapt and grow appears to have no bounds and one person's problem is another person's opportunity, therefore I think these challenges will be overcome.

• • • • •

2.6 Insights from Social Media Users

WHILE RESEARCHING THIS BOOK during 2007–2008, insights were gathered from

AskSteve.co

existing users of social media. What follows is a snapshot of what they thought of the four main opportunities that were discussed in the previous chapter.

The participants were women and men aged 35–55, working within a range of different service industries. A number of useful points came to light, the most compelling of which was said by practically all participants: although their organizations claimed to be open and transparent in their communication culture, they had failed to really achieve this in practice. An emerging theme was that there is little focus on any internal communication strategy or overall plan.

In Chapter 4, we will look at why it is imperative for any organization using social media to have a policy in place to govern its use. Chapter 5 provides a new tool, the Project Development Cycle, for planning and managing the implementation of social media in your organization.

2.6.1 Overview

Generally, the participants viewed both formal and informal communication methods as important and integral to effective working. Managers need not fear informal networks. They are perfectly natural and complement the desire of people to want to be in the know and to lobby for influence. These networks can be very strong and used by employees to disseminate an organization's *unwritten rules*. The unwritten rules set a pattern of acceptable behavior that toes the line of an organization's internal culture. This is, by definition, hard to pin down because of many factors, including how loose the rules are, the experience of the person interpreting the rules, the leadership regime that will judge an employee who breaks them, and the dynamic nature of the industry or internal conditions. The unwritten rules can manifest and grow from unknown sources. They can lead to unintended consequences that may serve neither the organization nor the employees well. The unwritten rules are regarded as an agreement to bend or break written policies if they get in the way of progress.

Often there is no direct relationship between management and most of the people with whom they are trying to communicate. *Testing the water* and upfront lobbying

SocialMediaInBusiness.com

through informal communication can smooth the path of any upcoming changes that need to be implemented and can also be less confrontational.

The general opinion from the survey was that formal structures within businesses may be too rigid. This can hinder effective decision-making. Using social media sites for informal communication can be effective in presenting feelers, collating ideas, and dealing with any objections. Furthermore, time is a valuable resource that can be more effectively used in a quick informal chat that gets to the heart of the matter.

The interviewees also felt that informal communication plays a key role in career progression and talent retention; that it is effectively a way to nurture relationships with key people within the organization. This is an aspect of organizational politics that will be discussed in more detail in Chapter 4.

Informal communication enables employees to learn the *shortcuts* to getting things done and through whom. These are things that are generally not written as policy. However, the process of discussing issues with colleagues also increases the sense of belonging and contributes to a feeling of greater job security.

Managers are often held accountable for internal communication but are very rarely responsible for it or in a strong position to influence it. They often act as mere *translators* for informal communication. Working from the middle of an organization, they are not regarded as having enough influence at the top of the organizational hierarchy. This makes it very difficult to gain enough trust from their employees. Social networks can bridge this gap if implemented properly. Just as an appropriate physical working environment and atmosphere is an important influence on informal communication, social networks can also provide these same opportunities in a virtual meeting space.

It was felt by many of the interviewees that not enough thought had gone into the design of online work environments, such as in-house intranets. By contrast, the social networks were constantly evolving to fulfill different communication needs. Using established social networks saves a company having to re-invent the wheel by trying to update an inadequate intranet. Building your informal networks wisely can make good things happen for your employees and your company.

AskSteve.co

2.6.2 Increase Visible Market Presence

Online social networks give the company the opportunity to build its business profile and increase its exposure to practically anyone; a teeming source of potential customers. The interviewees felt that social media enhanced the following aspects of business:

● Viral marketing

● Promotions to specific groups or communities

A Facebook fan page is an example of a social network that companies can use for this purpose.

2.6.3 Learning by Remote Training and Study

Social media can also be exploited to benefit managers by facilitating remote training, study groups, mentoring, and coaching. Below are examples of social media platforms that provide this service:

● **Webinars** – short for Web-based seminar. A presentation that can use video, text, and audio can be conducted using special software that can be rented on a subscription basis for around $50 a month (see gotowebinar.com).

● **Teleseminars** – This is a telephone audio conference that can be conducted on Skype (which is free). For cases where a large number of people are involved, there are specialized software platforms that can be purchased on a subscription basis for $30 a month (see instanttelesminar.com for a 21 day free trial).

● **Bookinars** – This provides an online seminar based on a book or paper, usually in the form of a series of online teleseminars, webinars, or a combination of the two. It is useful for remote learning and study groups (see Bookinars.co).

The key to these technologies is the marketing system, not the technology.

2.6.4 **Product Creation**

Social media enabled the interviewees to enhance their product creation process in the following ways:

- Introducing new product features
- Launching new products, gathering and analyzing feedback
- Facilitating beta trials, such as for software products or solutions
- Providing venues for pilot trials

YouTube is an example of a platform that benefits companies in this way.

2.6.5 **Enhancing Personal Reputation and Social Capital**

Social media helped the interviewees enhance the visibility of their personal profiles online. It led to an increase in exposure and access to other professionals in their field. It increased social capital, which is defined as the breadth and depth of one's contacts.

Your reputation can help your organization. Your presence online can help any party interested in your particular set of skills to locate and contact you easily. Your personal reputation can be built through contribution and reaching out to people not linked physically to you. Expert advice voluntarily given to unrelated parties can also boost your reputation in your particular field.

Social media allows the streamlining of contact management across different platforms and devices, such as smartphones and tablets. The mobile devices also enable you to manage Internet marketing activities and improve your rank on search engines.

The Institute of Directors, Ecademy for small business networks, and LinkedIn's university alumni groups are examples of social media sites useful for increasing social capital.

AskSteve.co

2.6.6 Relationship Building and Linking for Information and Expertise

In some cases this is as important as building assets. In fact, in some organizations, their assets are their employees. It stands to reason that building and maintaining a good relationship with new and existing contacts is an investment worth making. This is made more efficient by being online, where the organization can contact or be contacted very quickly. Offering expert advice is as beneficial to individuals as it is to their organizations. The Internet is loaded with expert advice, open source information, and applications that an organization can leverage to its advantage.

Good examples for relationship building are the Institute of Directors, LinkedIn, and Facebook Groups.

2.6.7 Recruitment, Resourcing, and Sourcing

Online exposure makes recruitment, resourcing, and sourcing more efficient. It provides access to an incredible number of potential employees and suppliers with a broad array of skills, wide ranging resources, and sources.

LinkedIn is an example network that provides many of these services.

2.6.8 Keeping in Touch with Colleagues and Reconnecting with Past Contacts

Being online makes it possible to keep in contact with business associates and acquaintances at any time of the day. It is widely regarded as essential to keep in touch with past contacts. For instance, it would be crucial to be able to contact former employees with very specific skills that were not efficiently transferred before their departure. Being online enables an organization to maintain these elusive links.

SocialMediainBusiness.com

Example networks good for these purposes are Facebook, LinkedIn, Ecademy, and Plaxo.

2.6.9 Project Collaboration

Collaboration can be achieved much more efficiently by being online. This is particularly important in cases where the needed parties are not located in one office. In addition, a group working on a particular project will have access to more people to bounce their ideas off of, encouraging cross fertilization of ideas with colleagues from within the organization or anyone else in the industry.

Example tools for collaborating on projects are YouSendIt, Dropbox, and Facebook Groups for conversation.

2.6.10 Being One Step Ahead of Formal Communication

The nature of online social networks makes it possible to know what is going on instantly and respond promptly.

Examples of this would be social network tools emulating a magazine or newspaper, and Google Reader.

2.6.11 Benefits of Social Networks over Intranets for Internal Communication

There was broad agreement among the interviewees that were familiar with social networks that they offered immense benefits and more features than simple business intranets. Below are their views on benefits and limitations.

- **Business Continuity; Disaster Recovery**
  Social networks enable users to respond quickly to issues and fast-moving events.

Companies can use these networks to communicate contingency plans in case of emergencies. If there was a disaster of some sort that made it impossible for staff to get to the office physically, they would know how to access information (such as contact numbers) and know what to do.

- **Enable Two-way Dialogue**
  Social networks provide a forum for improved dialogue, which could enable a better quality of decision-making. They allow the content of conversations to be controlled by the employees rather than the company, thereby humanizing the whole communication process.

- **Ease of Implementation**
  Social networks are easy to set up and use. The features are extremely user-friendly and intuitive. It might be beneficial to test a social media site like Facebook for yourself. This would allow you to better understand the social etiquette of this new environment. It would also allow you to discover any security issues that may arise and give you ways to identify solutions for your institution.

Below are some of the comments expressed during the interviews:

"The main impact is the globalization of business. We are talking about a big area… previously globalization was in the hands of a few big organizations with the resources. Now a company of any size (even a one-man band) has the capacity to go global in terms of building connections, profile, and marketing. It's about finding the right people to manage your business overseas. This makes it so much more accessible and enables small businesses to compete with large ones."

"Decisions are easier to make, processes made more efficient (e.g. if someone is going to go through a similar project in Australia as in England they can so much more easily share that information)."

"For me it means business travel is less daunting. I can connect with people far more easily through social networks. I'm going to New York next year and will be looking to fill my diary with meetings and with people to show me around."

"The impact is on the context and the culture of the company and how you want to dialogue with your stakeholders, the way the organization makes decisions, the style of management (open or closed), and broadcast versus dialogue style."

"Takes internal communications to the next level – makes it more personal."

"You can have a closer network on Facebook rather than an intranet."

"An intranet is controlled by the company (representing a central team or communications team with 50% content and 50% functions, but a centrally driven broadcast model). There is no real dialogue with another broadcast medium (that enables us saying exactly what we want to say) whereas…. we can pretend we are having dialogue."

• • • • •

AskSteve.co

2.7
Take Away Points

• • • • •

- Social networking technologies provide an enhanced way of mirroring offline communities in cyberspace. They provide an avenue to create new online communities with people who you might never meet in person in order to build strong, mutually beneficial relationships.

- The Internet landscape has drastically changed. As recently as 2008, the most popular application was MySpace; three years later, Facebook is the most popular social network. The fast-changing social media landscape means that managers have to keep an eye on this industry to understand how it is evolving. This will allow organizations to adapt their business procedures to match the changing ways that people interact with social media.

- New emerging principles of Web 2.0 (Tapscott and Williams, 2005) indicate that there is a fundamental shift emerging in the way the Internet is being used. A key trend of emerging technologies is towards more mobility for users. The way we are accessing the Internet is also changing. Some of the developments in mobility are tablet-computing technology, QR codes, and augmented reality. We are also accessing the Internet via our large flat screen televisions that provide new opportunities for business.

- Building on the four opportunities outlined in Chapter 1, the survey identified the following specific social media uses and advantages:

  - Build an organization's profile for awareness

  - Learning by remote training and study

  - Product creation

SocialMediaInBusiness.com

- Enhancing personal reputation and social capital
- Relationship building and linking for information and expertise
- Recruitment, resourcing, and sourcing
- Keeping in touch with colleagues and reconnecting with past contacts
- Finding information and sharing knowledge across groups
- Project collaboration
- Being one step ahead of formal communication
- Business continuity, disaster recovery
- Enabling two-way dialogue
- Ease of implementation

- The Internet, however, is not free. There is a cost incurred in maintenance and training that may impact the benefits you gain from social media. This is why unconventional innovative thinking is required to find that perfect combination of tools and strategies in order to achieve the most out of social media use.

- Fear of change is thought to be the greatest impediment for most businesses in embracing this new phenomenon. However, having a full understanding of its benefits, risks, and challenges is what will keep companies competitive and thriving. Chapter 4 will introduce you to some of the risks and challenges your organization may face.

• • • • •

CHAPTER 3

• • • • •

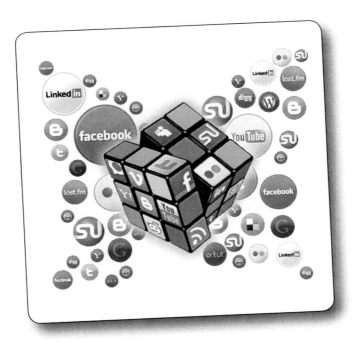

Social Media Applications Guide

THE PREVIOUS CHAPTER, Social Media Development, discussed how social media has evolved. This chapter outlines specific applications it offers through the lenses of the four opportunities discussed in Chapter 1: Communication, Communities, Collaboration, and Collective Intelligence.

Sixteen application categories (also called tools due to their essential functions) are revealed when we examine social media through these lenses; they are listed below. This list is certainly not exhaustive and is designed to give you a good feel for the landscape and the type of popular applications you might wish to explore. Social media applications are growing at an astounding rate as people are finding more and more ways to innovate. Following the table is a brief discussion of each one of the application categories, providing examples of specific popular applications (see Figure 20).

Communication	Communities
1. Meetings & Conferencing	5. Marketplaces
2. Sharing Media	6. Social Networks
3. Location Services	7. Blogs & Microblogs
4. Broadcasting	8. Virtual Worlds
Collaboration	**Collective Intelligence**
9. Freelance Platforms	13. Discussion Sites
10. Project & Team	14. Wikis
11. DIY Wiki Platforms	15. Ideas Platforms
12. DIY Social Networks	16. Market Intelligence

TABLE 2 • *Sixteen Application Categories*

SocialMediaInBusiness.com

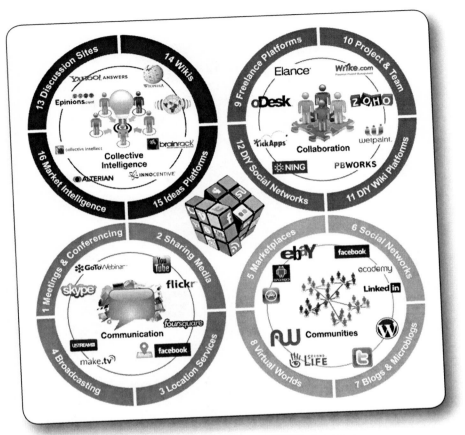

FIGURE 20 • *Social Media Applications Guide*

• • • • •

3.1 **Communication**

SOCIAL MEDIA APPLICATIONS that fall under the business opportunity of "Communication" enable users to: hold virtual meetings and conferences; share media such as documents, videos, audios, pictures, and slide presentations; find information where location is important, such as where the nearest cash machine is; and broadcast live video from a computer.

AskSteve.co

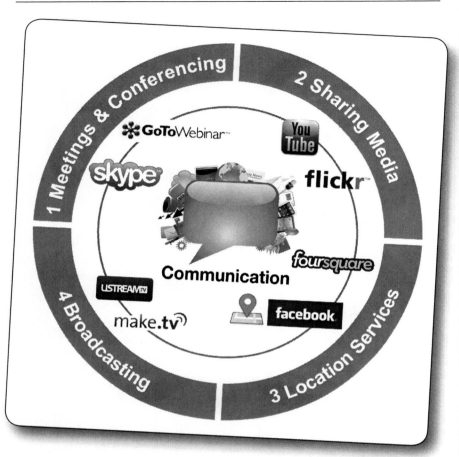

FIGURE 21 • *A Sample of Communication Applications*

3.1.1 **Meetings and Conferencing**

Online meetings or web conferences are meetings that occur through the use of the Internet as the medium of communication. These platforms can be used for one-on-one communication or for conferences between two or literally thousands of participants. This is cost-effective and convenient, since people from different parts of the world are able to conduct meetings without having to physically meet. Users can also share visuals like presentations, documents, and videos on computer screens, assisted by cloud computing services.

Meetings online can be conducted in a variety of methods. One of the most common methods is by creating a private chat room with audio overlay. Another way is to make use of a web conferencing provider. This is much more effective, since these providers have features that allow participants not only to verbally communicate with each other but also see each other virtually and record the meeting. Recording is especially useful for remote training purposes, to allow someone to catch up or allow a new member of your virtual team to review training materials. To get the best out of these tools, it is desirable to have some training and to develop effective processes.

POPULAR EXAMPLES

Skype (for up to 15 people)

On May 10, 2011, Skype announced they had been taken over by Microsoft for $8.5bn. As of July 2011, Skype had 663 million users worldwide, of which 124 million are active users. Skype is one of the most common means of communication used by businesses. It is a great way to connect with employees, suppliers, and customers. The free instant messaging, video calls, and video conferencing features are convenient and invaluable for different business transactions. It is also very easy to exchange any media with other users during the call. Placing calls between people who have Skype is free. Additionally, users can place calls to people who do not have Skype for a fee. The ability to see your list of contacts and their status, e.g. online, away, not available, do not disturb, makes impromptu meetings very easy.

GoToWebinar (for up to 1,000 people)

GoToWebinar enables users to carry out do-it-yourself webinars with up to 1,000 people for a flat rate. The software handles the registration of your users and provides automated email templates for marketing purposes. It also allows users to use customized branding and even do pre-webinar practice sessions. During the webinar, presenters can easily share presentation slides. The site features drawing tools, a pen, a spotlight, a highlighter, and arrow tools to encourage interaction with attendees. Presentation features such as audience view, dashboard, Q&A, and polls enable the audience to fully participate in the session. Webinars can

AskSteve.co

be a great way to conduct remote training. Webinars can be recorded and posted for those that could not make the meeting; this information can also be used for other purposes, such as blog posts, presentations, etc. Webinars can be good for generating more qualified leads and acquiring potential clients because a potential prospect gets to experience you for some considerable time (30-60 minutes).

3.1.2 Media Sharing

Social networks allow people to share media like images, texts, videos, and slide presentations across different platforms. One method of sharing media is for each user to download an application like Picasa in order to share photos. Another method is called cloud computing via services such as Apple iCloud, Amazon Web Services, or Google Docs. Finally, users can share media by uploading files to a specific online community or social network, YouTube for instance. It can then be shared with all visitors to the site or just specific people, depending on the preference of the user.

Internet marketers and business people regularly use social networks to share documents and video presentations with employees or possible clients. Online media sharing is a cheap and effective way to build brand recognition and promote the business. SlideShare is a popular site for sharing presentations and can be used to generate traffic to your website. For large file sharing, I recommend using Dropbox. This free and simple application allocates up to 2GB of space for creating folders of shared material – especially useful when working with a freelancer or working on small projects, for example when you need someone overseas to work on your presentation slides.

POPULAR EXAMPLES

YouTube

YouTube is probably the most popular media-sharing site available today. Millions of people visit YouTube every day. YouTube statistics claim that the site exceeds two million views per day, nearly double the primetime audience of all four major U.S. broadcast networks combined. These statistics prove that using this tool could be a huge opportunity for businesses to connect with existing and new customers. Creating a YouTube channel for your business is highly recommended and is very easy. Additionally, there are many videos explaining how to do it. The key benefit is that it creates traffic to your website or blog. The Holy Grail for any business is to have a video go "viral," in other words, to become popular through Internet sharing and generate large volumes of traffic to your site. Advertising agencies typically are trying to create viral campaigns in the consumer market, and it is worth looking at the top viral videos.

A software application called Jing, by TechSmith, is very useful for recording and editing your screen, and it is free. A more powerful version with more features by the same company is called Camtasia.

Flickr

Flickr is an online sharing application and photo management tool that helps users organize and share pictures and videos quickly, easily, and free of charge. Pro accounts are available for users who want to upload and display high volumes of pictures. Flickr is a good way of generating traffic to your website or blog and interacting with employees and customers. Photobucket is another popular application similar to Flickr.

3.1.3 Location Services

Location services are software applications for web-enabled mobile devices. They work by detecting the location of the user through their mobile device. This contextual information then allows the service provider to send relevant information based on the user's location, such as the location of the nearest bank or coffee shop. You can also share your location with your contacts and friends if you choose. The service provider can send a map with relevant information to the user's mobile phone. Location services also allow businesses to attract new customers when they are listed on location-based social networks like Foursquare. This gives them an opportunity to attract more customers, increase revenue, and more importantly, reward loyalty.

POPULAR EXAMPLES

Foursquare

Foursquare is a location-based mobile platform that allows users to explore cities while earning points and badges along the way. Users must "check in" at venues by running the program on their mobile devices and selecting from a list of venues that the program locates nearby. They can then share that location with other users. Merchants or brands optimize the Foursquare platform by utilizing its diverse set of tools to attract and retain customers. Some businesses provide incentives for the most frequent customer. In Foursquare, the most frequent customer is designated "The Mayor." For instance, the JD Wetherspoon chain of pubs in the UK provides a 20% discount on food for the Mayor of any of its public houses, rewarding their most loyal customers.

Facebook Places

Facebook has created its own location-based service called Facebook Places. In October 2010, only two months after Facebook Places was launched, over 20 million members worldwide had tried the Facebook Places service.

Facebook Places lets the user see where their friends are currently "checked in" nearby. It allows users to share their whereabouts anytime, anywhere. It also allows tagging friends in the places the user visits, viewing comments, and earning quirky merit badges and coupons. What is unique about Facebook Places is its range of privacy controls. It lets the user have the power over the location information they wish to share and with whom they want to share it.

3.1.4 Broadcasting

Broadcasting or webcasting refers to dispersing a single communication to the general public or wide audience at the same time, live.

Webcasting is broadcasting live audio and video transmissions via the Intranet or Internet. Companies can enhance productivity by using social media applications that specialize in webcasting. It provides an efficient way of broadcasting initiatives

SocialMediaInBusiness.com

to customers, reaching a wide audience, working around time-sensitive issues, and carrying out interactive question and answer sessions. It also creates ways to access potential buyers, build brand awareness, and increase sales.

It is less costly to engage in webcasting than attempt to target each segment of consumers using individualized marketing communication. Typically, users can register for free and are then given access to basic features. Upgrading the membership for a cost provides more services, such as unlimited airtime, more file storage, and an unlimited number of viewers. Receiving webcast content is also simple. It is usually accomplished by using RealPlayer or Windows Media Player. Both applications are free for download.

POPULAR EXAMPLES

Make.tv and Ustream.tv

Make.tv and Ustream.tv are two sites that focus on webcasting recorded and live events. Make.tv allows the user to produce and design a show to broadcast over the Internet. The user can also broadcast real-time conferences and videos online. Many people create a regular series of useful information for their subscribers; creativity is the name of the game.

Ustream.tv allows the user to watch and interact with shows around the world in real time and broadcast information from mobile phones or computers.

Webcasting allows companies to promote their business in a more interactive, engaging, and affordable way. Using this tool allows companies to reduce travel costs, improve communication, and develop sustainable business practices.

● ● ● ● ●

AskSteve.co

3.2 **Communities**

SOCIAL MEDIA APPLICATIONS that fall under the business opportunity of "Communities" are the markets, the communities, and the groups where you will find your customers, suppliers, and competitors. This is the evolving marketplace. Broadly speaking, the types of communities are marketplaces, social networks, blogs, microblogs, and virtual worlds.

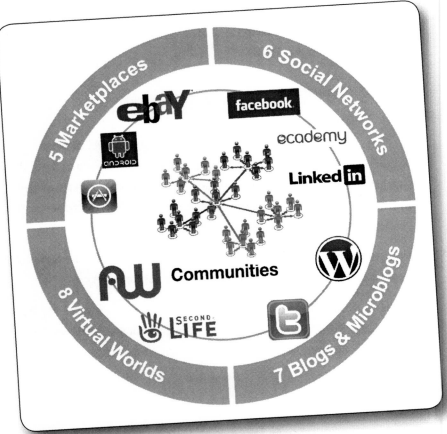

FIGURE 22 • *A Sample of Communities Applications*

3.2.1 Marketplaces

An online marketplace is a site built around e-commerce; the buying and selling of a variety of goods between users on the site. Most online marketplaces have user-friendly features. They offer a simple interface where sellers can easily list items they have for sale, where buyers can browse and buy, and where a mechanism for collection of payment is also available. Users only have to enter their payment information (credit cards, debit cards, PayPal accounts) and the mechanics of the transfer of funds are taken care of. Online marketplaces provide an avenue for businesses to increase sales revenue without much overhead cost. Using popular online marketplaces allows companies to instantly reach millions of new customers around the world and generate traffic to their website.

POPULAR EXAMPLES

Apple Store and Android Market

The rising trend of applications (apps) for mobile devices has given birth to online marketplaces for the sale of these apps. Instead of having to comb the Internet to find an application that a business requires, app stores help streamline the shopping process by providing a hub where users can browse and buy the apps they need. Spearheaded by Apple, mobile app stores have flourished since consumers began valuing the convenience and functionality brought about by either free or paid mobile applications.

There are new apps coming out every day that mirror the social media applications. They seek to extend your desktop to your mobile device and to make it easier to sync the mobile and the desktop (e.g. LogMeIn Ignition and Evernote). Popular applications such as Facebook, LinkedIn, YouTube, Twitter, Skype, and Groupon all now have a mobile version of their site. It may be appropriate to have a mobile app for your business site to make access from a mobile device easier for your customers. Use of a QR code, as discussed in the previous chapter, may also be appropriate.

eBay Auction Site

The eBay marketplace is a practical online platform where businesses and individuals sell a variety of products and services. According to eBay, more than 94 million people use their site every day. This number makes it the world's largest online marketplace. Browsing through items listed for sale does not require a user account. An account is, however, needed in order to buy or sell items. Items can be purchased through bidding in auction-style sales, or by paying a fixed price in order to purchase an item immediately. Localized sites in the United States, Canada, and the United Kingdom have also been created for a more community-based trading experience. The sheer popularity of eBay makes it a valuable tool for businesses seeking another outlet for sales and for driving traffic to your site. Again, creativity is the name of the game.

3.2.2 Social Networks

Social networks allow a particular company to easily connect with suppliers, customers, and other key individuals or organizations. Business social networks work by registering with a specific site, such as Facebook or LinkedIn. Once an individual or organization is registered, other users of the same social network can be added. The user can search for specific people or organizations that are registered with the social networking site and send a request to be connected with these people/organizations.

There are some very successful local social networking sites, such as QQ and Baidu in China, Orkut in Brazil, and Hi5 in Thailand. However, their success is limited to specific countries.

Managers can use social networks to extend their reach, create branding opportunities, and improve communication with suppliers and customers. There are many other benefits of business-oriented social networking sites, but the ultimate goal is to improve business.

POPULAR EXAMPLES

Facebook

Facebook is the leading social networking website today and could fit into nearly all the categories of applications; such is the scope and ambition of Facebook. Although it is far more than a social network, social networking is at the core of Facebook's offerings. Facebook is an evolving social network with thousands of applications operating within the platform through an ecosystem of developers, all of which must interwork with Facebook.

Founded in 2004, Facebook aims to connect family, friends, and business associates by integrating email, chat/instant messaging, photo and video sharing, and more. As of January 2011, Facebook had over 600 million active users (Business Insider, 2011).

Having a Facebook strategy is now necessary for many businesses because it is a market of 600 million people and therefore accessing that market effectively is a must. Developing such a strategy is beyond the scope of this book because Facebook justifies a book in its own right. This subject is discussed in some depth in the training courses provided on www.SocialMediaInBusiness.com/Training.

A business can create a unique presence on Facebook (fan page) and provide links to the company's website. Facebook makes it possible for organizations to target customers by tailoring ads that appear in each user's profile. This can be an extremely cost-effective advertising strategy and can be tried at low risk. Facebook is fantastic for creating awareness of your company or brand and can be used for generating leads, building your sales list, increasing sales, generating insight into your customers, or conducting customer service surveys. Facebook provides a lot of customer analytics that can be very useful for feedback and for measuring your progress.

Facebook has even got its own currency called Facebook Credits for purchasing virtual goods and apps, which became mandatory on all gaming sites on Facebook after July 1, 2011. Facebook has launched group buying, called "buy with friends." This is currently only for virtual goods. It is possible that the currency could be expanded to cover other physical goods in the future.

The biggest cost associated with Facebook is the cost of time required in gaining the appropriate knowledge and experience to get the best out of it.

Ecademy

Ecademy is a social network geared toward the networking and support needs of small to medium businesses. The site offers many features to help business people connect with one another and provides an avenue for organizations to build an online presence. Members can send messages to other members and build up followers by writing blogs. In addition, any events that companies might be holding can be posted on the site's event calendar to generate traffic. Products can also be listed for sale on the site's marketplace. As an additional benefit, the site offers resources like the Ecademy Digital School, where members can get help with adapting their business to the Internet. Basic membership is free but gives users access to only a limited number of features. A fee is required in order to access more features on the site.

Ecademy has a combination of online and local offline meetings to enable members to meet face-to-face at networking events; their initial aim was a friend in every city, and now their motto is: *Know me, Like me, Follow me.*

One to watch is the new social network called Google+ from Google. The key features of this are "Circles," which enable you to segment your contacts; "Hangouts," which informs your contacts you are available for a chat online; "Sparks," which looks for videos and articles that it thinks you will like; and "Huddle," which enables group chat. This could be serious competition for Facebook, but is in fact Google's third attempt at reaching Facebook's audience.

3.2.3 Blogs and Microblogs

A blog can be a stand-alone website or a part of a bigger website. It is a place where a person can share their thoughts and media, like pictures, videos, and audios. A microblog is a much shorter blog. A microblog entry could just be a sentence fragment, picture, or video. This is also popular among businesses that are trying to increase revenue. Twitter tends to be used by other applications, such as Tweetdeck (recently acquired by Twitter) and HootSuite, as part of a growing Twitter ecosystem.

Creating a blog is easy because of different web-based platforms like WordPress, Blogger, TypePad, and many others. The platforms allow "plug-in" tools that are provided free by an ecosystem of independent developers and have additional features for a price. Blogs get higher rankings and quicker indexing, which means you are more visible. They create brand awareness. They enhance customer relationship management by informing people of available services and products, and help you gain insights into your customers through comments and feedback.

Position your company as an industry expert by using blogs. Apart from writing updates and information about your company, include useful facts that can inform, educate, assist, and entertain readers. Consolidate valuable and interesting content from other industries that are related to your field. This way, readers will follow your blog and look to you as a good resource and expert in the field. Another strategy is to develop relationships with other well-known and successful bloggers related to your industry by creating an occasional blog post for them. This can optimize your company's exposure by "back-linking" the blog post to your website.

POPULAR EXAMPLES

WordPress

WordPress is one of the most popular free blogging tools available online. It has a powerful content management system that allows users to do more than just blogging. WordPress is also a great tool for building a business website. Its editing interface is easy to use, allowing users to create and update contents like blog posts and web pages without knowing any programming language. By using just a web browser, the process of creating and editing pages only involves a simple text editor, similar to using Microsoft Word.

WordPress has a booming ecosystem of developers creating plug-ins and customizable themes. Users can take advantage of the pre-existing design themes or add features like polls, ratings, contact forms, and more.

WordPress also offers good search engine optimization (SEO) and social media integration. Additional features can be added automatically, requiring little or no effort. It is advisable to get help setting it up, but once set up it is relatively easy to use. There is a vast array of freelance website designers who are willing to help. They are available via freelance websites such as Elance.com.

Twitter

Twitter is the most popular microblogging service today. By the end of 2010, it had over 175 million registered users generating 75 million posts or tweets per day. Twitter allows users to stay updated with the latest information about what they find interesting. The core of this real-time information network is the "tweets" consisting of up to 140 characters in length. Twitter is a great social networking site that allows companies to reach out to customers and potential clients. Twitter serves as a tool in achieving successful customer relationship management through social media marketing.

IBM uses Twitter to provide interactive communication with customers. Over 1,000 IBM employees worldwide "tweet" with each other and their customers on a daily basis, thus the company has easy-to-obtain word-of-mouth marketing and easy networking.

Dell Outlet uses Twitter to "tweet" major promotions and discounts for Dell products. In 2009, Twitter helped Dell's retail chain sales surpass $2 million, a dramatic improvement.

3.2.4 **Virtual Worlds**

A virtual world is an online community that intends for its users to inhabit, interact, and create objects in cyberspace. The users often take the form of avatars, cartoon-like characters in a computer-simulated environment through which the user is visible to others graphically. Visual gestures, text, graphical icons, sound and voice commands, and touch sensations can be used to communicate with other users. If holographic technology ever comes into its own, this technology will become commonplace.

The virtual world is generally well known for its ability to allow users to explore a whole new world of playing online games. However, the virtual world is not only created for online gamers or merely to let the imagination soar, but it also involves marketplaces, real business, and profit making. I would suggest this is a more advanced strategy in the social media landscape. However, the virtual world might be where your target market is located, so it cannot be ignored.

- **Advertising** – Using virtual worlds in business settings enables companies to access a specific clientele and customer demographic. For example, Apple created an online store within Second Life that allows online users to browse their new, innovative products. Users cannot actually buy a product, but "virtual stores" contribute to brand or product awareness and online presence.

- **Generating Feedback** – Virtual worlds are a good environment for testing user reaction. Receiving feedback and insights as to what the real market and buyers want from new products can give an organization a competitive advantage and a better understanding of the target market.

- **Training** – In a virtual world it is possible to create training environments, for instance, to learn a language. The users can be transported to a scenario of being in a restaurant to learn and practice their language skills.

POPULAR EXAMPLES

Second Life

Second Life is the largest user-created 3D virtual community on the Internet. Basic membership is free but premium memberships are also available for a price. Premium memberships offer additional features, like a private virtual home, sign-up bonus, and weekly rewards.

There are many interesting things to do in this virtual world. The user can create an avatar, explore different places, and interact with other users. The user can even make money, buy things, and purchase virtual properties. Text and voice chat is available for interaction with other users, allowing organizations to hold meetings.

AskSteve.co

Active Worlds (3D World Creator)

In a nutshell, Active Worlds is a do-it-yourself version of Second Life, where you create your own world from components that already exist or ones you have custom-made. The key advantage is "your world – your rules," whereas with Second Life the world exists but the rules are set by Linden Corporation, the owners of Second Life. Active Worlds is a popular 3D virtual reality platform where users are able to create their own virtual characters, explore different 3D virtual environments that other users have built, and interact with other users. Users can chat with each other and build their own environments. "Tourist Mode" allows interested parties to enjoy this virtual reality for free.

• • • • •

3.3 **Collaboration**

SOCIAL MEDIA APPLICATIONS that fall under the business opportunity of "Collaboration" enable users to collaborate: use freelance skills; work in projects and teams; create DIY wikis; and create DIY social networks.

3.3.1 **Freelance Platforms**

Freelance platforms are a breakthrough in the outsourcing of programmers, designers, writers, translators, marketers, researchers, and admin contractors – to name a few of the skills available. These are online marketplaces that provide cost-effective ways of hiring capable freelancers or contractors locally or globally for duties such as administrative support, engineering and manufacturing, and design and multimedia. These platforms draw web traffic in the hundreds of thousands each month, which translates into a huge pool of skilled professionals that organizations can hire to work on projects. An important part of these systems is contractors are rated by clients, who also provide testimonials and feedback. Some show earnings and number of projects completed.

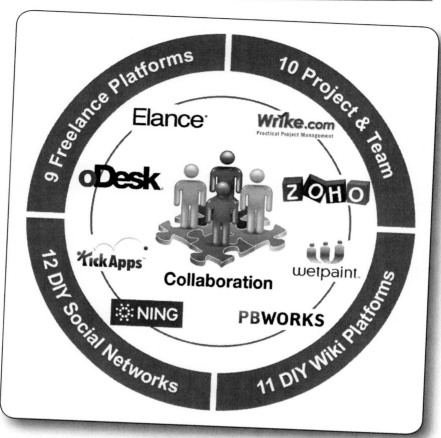

FIGURE 23 • *A Sample of Collaboration Applications*

Many freelance platforms are free to join and others require a low membership fee. These sites aim to present a user-friendly experience with easy transactions between employers and contractors. The process of posting projects, choosing the best bid, hiring a contractor, and paying for the completed project is usually very intuitive. Skype and Dropbox are also useful tools to use when working with freelance contractors; it is easy to communicate and share documents effectively, especially given the different time zones. When dealing with freelancers from other cultures, communication has to take into account the different cultural practices that can be frustrating if you are not used to dealing with people from different parts of the world. Many of the things we take for granted in our own culture can be quite

different elsewhere. Make sure both parties fully understand what is required for the job in question, including deadlines and fees.

Freelance platforms allow managers to bring in specialist skills and temporary skills in a time and cost-efficient way, and to arrange payment on a project basis or to pay hourly. Managers can access thousands of freelancers without sifting through various job sites and classified ads. Through freelance hiring, companies also minimize their operational costs, since there is no need to pay a monthly salary, benefits, bonuses, or incentives. One example is Amazon's Mechanical Turk (mturk.com), which is one of the most popular Freelance platforms in the USA but is currently only available in that country. Instead, I will focus upon two global freelance platforms: Elance and oDesk.

POPULAR EXAMPLES

Elance

Elance is a freelance site that is based in California and has existed since 1999. This platform allows outsourcing companies and a talent pool of more than 100,000 freelancers to come together. Clients or potential employers are allowed to post projects or job openings, invite freelancers to make a bid, and select the freelancer with the best expertise and proposal.

Elance provides a workroom for each project to facilitate collaboration and enable effective communication between the employer and the freelancer. The client only pays for the work that the contractor performs; at a rate that is agreed upon before work begins. A typical project might range between $50 and $500. Elance offers guaranteed payment of work done by holding funds in escrow until the project is completed to the satisfaction of both parties. Elance also offers convenient modes of payment; freelancers have the option of linking their Elance account with their bank account for wire transfers, as needed.

oDesk

oDesk is similar to Elance in that employers can post jobs and hire contractors to work on projects. oDesk also offers the employer the ability to conduct interviews before hiring freelancers.

Portfolios, proposals, work histories, feedback, and ratings play an important role in allowing employers to select the most qualified contractor. oDesk displays this relevant information to assist employers in decision-making during the selection process. oDesk also guarantees automated time-tracking, progressive results, and close monitoring of contractors.

The oDesk payment system is secure, accurate, and streamlined. Weekly financial reports and contractors' work diaries can be viewed for auditing purposes. oDesk also has built-in messaging and chatting systems to enable all parties to communicate effectively.

3.3.2 Project and Team

Technological advances mean that employees are no longer confined to the four walls of their respective offices. Collaboration is now possible with the use of online document management systems, mobile phones, laptops, and other similar devices. This is all possible with the aid of the different online collaboration tools available today. These tools allow managers, project supervisors, and employees to:

- Easily keep track of projects

- Communicate with each other regardless of physical location

- Submit reports from various locations

- Streamline the work process

- Access files and important documents from different locations

Online collaboration tools offer diverse features and specialties to help companies connect their teams across silos. Managers only need to choose the right tool – the one that suits their organization's needs.

POPULAR EXAMPLES

Wrike

Wrike's project management features are useful in managing multiple projects from one online workspace. It provides managers with the

AskSteve.co

ability to see the "bigger picture" in regard to all projects currently on the go. It also helps with day-to-day tasks, such as reminders and scheduling. The site also allows project documents to be stored online in order for employees to access them easily from anywhere. Thousands of teams from all over the world make use of Wrike's intuitive project management features.

This site requires a subscription, with fees starting from $49 a month for a team of five members. There is, however, a free trial available for companies interested in trying it on for size.

 Zoho

Zoho is a popular collaboration site that provides a wide range of useful applications for businesses. It boasts over 4 million users to date. According to the website, "Zoho.com offers a comprehensive suite of award-winning online business, productivity & collaboration applications. Customers use Zoho Applications to run their business processes, manage their information and be more productive while at the office or on the go, without having to worry about expensive or outdated hardware or software" (Zoho.com, 2011).

There are over 20 different applications available. They include project management applications, invoicing, and web conferencing tools. These applications are free for individuals but require subscription fees for organizations.

Zoho enables individuals and businesses to systematically manage documents and streamline the work process while significantly reducing operational costs.

3.3.3 DIY Wiki Platforms

The rising popularity of wikis, such as Wikipedia, has encouraged many companies to build wikis internally to help facilitate information sharing, collaboration, and better project management.

Wiki platforms are tools used to develop a user-created encyclopedia. Generally, they are used as project management tools, but these platforms also provide other benefits, such as improved documentation and customer or client collaboration.

DIY wiki platforms allow users to share information with other users on a central site. Collaborators are able to share articles, spreadsheets, text, RSS feeds, and videos with each other.

POPULAR EXAMPLES

PBworks

PBworks, formerly known as PBwiki, is a commercial collaborative editing platform in real-time format. With over 1 million team workspaces, it is by far the world's largest provider of hosted collaboration business solutions. PBworks serves millions of users every month, including big companies like AT&T, Cisco, FedEx, and Citi.

This site is a good starting point for users without wiki experience. It only features two tabs: "view," used for read-only viewing, and "edit" to make changes and deletions. It also allows users to add content by clicking the "Insert Plugin" button. Users can add video and Google Gadgets, as well as upload files like spreadsheets and calendars. PBworks offers basic features for free. Advanced features are also available for a price.

Wetpaint

Wikis by Wetpaint (www.wetpaintcentral.com) is a platform that seeks to provide low-cost content based on social publishing. It has an intuitive interface similar to blogs and offers users the option of monitoring wiki activity. Wikis by Wetpaint reaches 10 million unique users every month. It is designed on a simple permission system given to various users – creator, administrator, or registered user (either writer or moderator), to create their own wikis.

3.3.4 DIY Social Networks

"White label" social networking platforms allow companies to create their own social networks (usually from scratch). This is a great option for companies with specific requirements who do not wish to use popular social media sites, or want to store their own "internal" knowledge for security reasons. They offer the flexibility

AskSteve.co

companies need to create specific marketing and communication tools that sites like Facebook do not have. These DIY sites often allow companies to integrate their own applications into the platform. In choosing a DIY network, managers will be wise to consider the specific features needed, as different platforms offer different features and applications. Managers must also determine the ease of implementing the network into the organization and ensure that security measures are in place to protect the flow of information across the network.

POPULAR EXAMPLES

Ning

Ning is a DIY social networking platform that provides the most professional, user-friendly tools for setting up visually appealing and fully functional social networks from scratch. Ning's standard package is available for a reasonable cost, allowing companies to build an ad-supported social network site using the functional features that the site offers. The process is easy. It includes a point-and-click process to customize the look of their site and add features like photos, videos, chat, blogs, Ning apps, and groups. In a matter of a few minutes, users can create a social network and can immediately accept members.

KickApps

KickApps is designed not for beginners but more for web developers, as well as companies having web developers on staff. This DIY social networking platform is suitable for the integration of social networking features into a company's existing site, eliminating the inconvenience of creating a network from scratch. Unlike Ning, KickApps requires the developer to have full control over the aesthetic features, including header and footer code and CSS styling.

Without paying a fee, users are allowed to customize their network's URL and enjoy unlimited storage and bandwidth encompassing all multimedia content, such as audio, video, and photos. KickApps also provides a full-bodied set of widget creation tools, allowing organizations to promote their networks via viral marketing. Widgets embedded on different sites can drive traffic to an organization's website.

3.4 Collective Intelligence

SOCIAL MEDIA APPLICATIONS that fall under the business opportunity of "Collective Intelligence" enable users to engage in discussion, access wikis, participate and share ideas, and gain market intelligence. Each category will be discussed in brief.

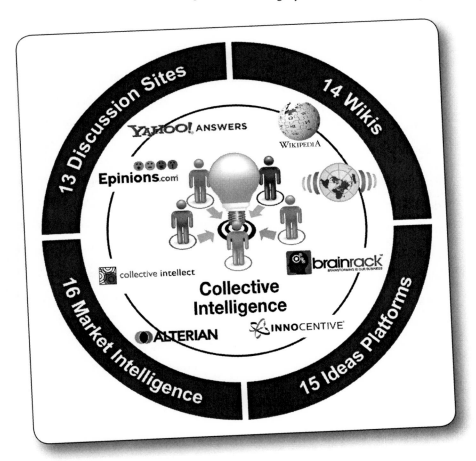

FIGURE 24 • *A Sample of Collective Intelligence Applications*

3.4.1 Discussion Sites

Discussion sites include question and answer sites as well as sites where users post product or service reviews and ratings.

Question and answer sites are exactly that – a forum where users post a question online and members provide informative answers. Most question and answer sites require users to set up a free account before they are able to ask or answer questions. User ratings ensure the quality of answers that members give. Certain websites such as Helium and WebAnswers also offer a financial reward to people who have given the best answer to a particular question.

From a business perspective, question and answer sites are an avenue that an organization can use to generate brand awareness. Answering questions allows that company to become known as an expert in its field (particularly in professional forums, such as LinkedIn Answers). Proper answers to queries that are related to your industry can also bring in potential buyers and repeat customers.

Positive reviews and ratings have always been a powerful influence in a buyer's decision-making process (e.g. Amazon for their products and TripAdvisor for hotels). The collective intelligence of previous customer opinions influences future customer choices. Companies may spend thousands of dollars on marketing, but without the support of positive reviews, buyers may not purchase a product. In fact, most people rely on user reviews for product information or research before a buying decision is made. This results in an increased volume of sales of products that are positively reviewed. There is a corresponding drop-off on the sales of products with poor consumer ratings. Most reviews and ratings sites are free to use and are easily accessible to the public.

POPULAR EXAMPLES

Yahoo!

Yahoo! Answers is an example of a question and answer site with a simple 3-step how-to guide: 1. Ask. 2. Answer. 3. Discover. An account is required before the user can post or answer questions. Registration for the service is free.

SocialMediaInBusiness.com

Members can ask any question, provided it is not offensive and respects the site's user guidelines. The question remains open for four to eight days to receive answers.

Members can also browse the archive of answered questions and discover a wealth of ideas, expertise, and experiences that people have shared.

Epinions

Established in 1999, Epinions is a popular consumer review site. The site aims to help people make informed buying decisions by providing in-depth product reviews and recommendations. Epinions offers monetary and non-monetary incentives to encourage users to post reviews. There is no form of censorship on this network; as such, both good and bad reviews can be posted to give people an unbiased report of a particular product or service. Each review features the pros, cons, and the reviewer's "bottom line" assessment of the product. A person wishing to submit reviews must first register for free with the site.

3.4.2 Wikis

Wikis are sites where people from all over the world can contribute and edit articles about certain topics.

Since this platform is open to the general public, there is the possibility that articles may contain errors. And it must be said that there have been isolated cases of large companies polishing articles to make them look good by removing the negatives. This strategy rarely works because on the Internet there is always someone watching, and getting caught creates a lot of negative press. Most sites try to combat this issue by asking editors to ensure that only factual information is posted. However, used correctly, the benefits of this social network outweigh the risks for most individuals and businesses. It provides managers with easy access to information. Organizations can also use this platform to publish information about their mission and products or services, thereby building brand awareness and reaching a large audience.

POPULAR EXAMPLES

Wikipedia

Wikipedia is known to be the biggest online encyclopedia collection of all time. As of January 2010, Wikipedia had over 17 million articles, all written by volunteers and available in more than 270 languages. Wikipedia is so popular that in January 2011, according to comScore, it made the list of the ten most visited sites in the United States. A user account is required in order to create an article, but most articles may be edited with or without a user account.

Wikinews

Wikinews is a site focused on current news events. Its users submit all the articles, with each article concentrating on a single event. Wikinews encourages its users to submit articles that are factual, written without bias, and that aim to present all points of view. Articles do not only have one author; it is a collaborative effort, with users from around the world editing the stories in order to achieve a good end result.

3.4.3 Ideas Platforms

Idea sharing networks provide a platform where different individuals can come together to brainstorm ideas in order to solve problems. The ingenious concept of idea sharing networks has helped countless businesses all over the world. It is a cost-effective and convenient way to share ideas and resolve challenges. These platforms target specific market areas, including:

- **Research and development networks** – These networks focus on helping companies by providing solutions to research and development problems.

- **Prediction platforms** – These are sites where a company can get an educated prediction about industry trends to help with its decision-making process.

- **Online advocacy and fundraising sites** – Allow companies to get involved with different community initiatives. Sponsoring specific causes is also a great way of increasing awareness for a company.

SocialMediaInBusiness.com

- **Crowd-funding platforms** – These sites bring together a group of people who pitch in to support a specific idea or business. This is particularly useful to small companies that need capital quickly and where a bank may not be inclined to fund them.

POPULAR EXAMPLES

InnoCentive

InnoCentive is an open innovation firm that focuses on aiding companies in acquiring fast solutions to research and development problems. They use crowdsourcing to solve organizations' challenges in areas such as math, chemistry, computer science, engineering, physical sciences, and life sciences.

InnoCentive operates a global network of over 200,000 potential problem solvers and offers cash prizes ranging from $5,000–$1,000,000, depending on the challenge. An example would be the unique challenges posed by space exploration at NASA. As discussed in Chapter 1, a group of independent experts is more likely to come up with a better result than a team of experts working together as one. InnoCentive uses this at the center of their business approach. They protect the intellectual property issues by only showing the solution to the company, InnoCentive, and the solution provider.

How does it work? The company posts its challenge and gets a series of proposals to the challenge. InnoCentive offers this example: Roche had a challenge that had been ongoing for 15 years. Within two months of posting on InnoCentive, they had 1,000 unique solvers signed on to the project and a total of 113 proposals; it was solved in 60 days. Interestingly, all the solutions Roche had tried over the 15 years had come in as proposals.

Brainrack

Brainrack is unique in that it encourages students to come up with solutions to challenges that companies place. The student with the best solution wins the prize money. If more than one solution is chosen, those students split the prize money evenly.

AskSteve.co

Ideas remain confidential and can only be seen by the company submitting the challenge, known as the "host." The host has a maximum of eight weeks to review and rank the submitted solutions and select a winner. The company may also invite the winners for a job interview or internship based on the competencies they observed in the submitted proposals.

3.4.4 Market Intelligence

Market intelligence tools show the overall evaluation of a given global market using economic and social statistics, such as demographics, population data, and total consumption levels. Market intelligence tools provide the "bigger picture" for companies to better understand the environment in which they are competing. These tools also help business owners understand and take advantage of opportunities for the business, minimize the probable threats, and plan strategic actions necessary to succeed.

Building in-house market intelligence tools requires spending more resources than many companies can afford. Using social media sites that provide these features is a more cost-effective option for most organizations. If you are not monitoring what is being said about your company, products, and services, you will not be able to respond effectively. Trendrr (www.trendrr.com) is an example of a business intelligence tool to "listen to the web."

People-search applications are useful services to carry out background checks on potential clients, suppliers, and new employees. These tools are useful for managing your online profile. They are simple and easy to use: just type in the name and location. Popular examples are Pipl and kgbpeople.

POPULAR EXAMPLES

Alterian
The goal of Alterian is to create effective, useful, and engaging marketing campaigns to help organizations reinforce customer loyalty.

Their goal is to transform traditional marketing and communication functions into a practical, cost-effective strategy to achieve multichannel engagement with a company's target market.

According to the website, the Alterian platform integrates email, social media monitoring, campaign management, and web content management tools to help managers achieve a more insightful and targeted marketing campaign. Alterian works with more than 150 agencies, system integrators, and marketing services partners who understand the necessity to plan and implement coordinated customer engagement services along with their customers.

Collective Intellect

Collective Intellect is a site that aims to monitor and analyze social media data so that companies can engage with customers more effectively. The site guides companies towards understanding what customers want to hear, the topics in which potential clients are most interested, or platforms they would rather use. Collective Intellect guides companies as they embrace the integration of social media analytics into their business processes.

In an aggressively competitive industry, having good market intelligence will give an organization the competitive edge. Managers need to research their industry in order to understand the purchasing patterns of their target market. This knowledge will help businesses develop their brand in relation to consumer behavioral patterns. This is a key ingredient to business success.

The applications listed in Chapter 3 are also available in electronic form with clickable links and four tables of links to further examples (The Social Media Applications Guide – Ebook).
Go to www.SocialMediaInBusiness.com/Store

● ● ● ● ●

AskSteve.co

3.5
Take Away Points

• • • • •

- Given how quickly social media has exploded onto the scene for businesses, it is no surprise that the possibilities can seem overwhelming. Using the four key business opportunities explained in this chapter, it is possible to narrow the field to sixteen widely available applications or tools that businesses can easily use to their advantage.

- Managers are only limited by their biases or fears when it comes to the opportunities that social media applications afford.

- Because individual employees are likely to be familiar with one or more of these applications, there is an obvious strategy available to managers that would see staff members taking the lead, as individuals or in teams, to introduce and consult with colleagues on these various possibilities.

Communication	Communities	Collaboration	Collective Intelligence
1. Meetings & Conferencing *Skype* *GoToWebinar*	5. Marketplaces *Apple Store* *eBay*	9. Freelance Platforms *Elance* *oDesk*	13. Discussion Sites *Yahoo! Answers* *Epinions*
2. Media Sharing *YouTube* *Flickr*	6. Social Networks *Facebook* *Ecademy*	10. Project Team Collaboration *Wrike* *Zoho*	14. Wikis *Wikipedia* *Wikinews*
3. Location-Based Services *Foursquare* *Facebook*	7. Blogs & Microblogs *WordPress* *Twitter*	11. DIY Wiki Platforms *PBworks* *Wetpaint*	15. Ideas sharing *InnoCentive* *Brainrack*
4. Broadcasting *Make.tv* *Ustream.tv*	8. Virtual Worlds *Second Life* *Active Worlds*	12. DIY Social Networks *Ning* *KickApps*	16. Market Intelligence *Alterian* *Collective Intellect*

TABLE 3 • *Sixteen Categories of Social Media and 32 Examples*

SocialMediaInBusiness.com

CHAPTER 4

• • • • •

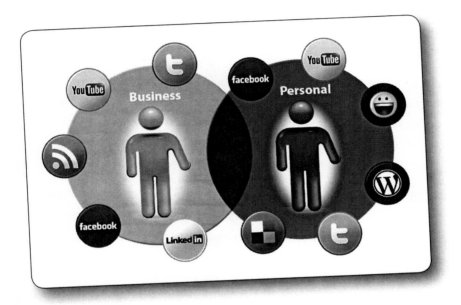

Social Media:
The Dark Side

4.1 **Introduction**

CHAPTER 2 REFERRED TO A SAMPLE STUDY of women and men aged 35–55 working within a range of different service industries that has revealed a number of valuable insights. Key among those insights were certain fears expressed by the participants about the use of social media. This chapter will examine the risks and challenges in social media that have to be managed, and the most effective ways to mitigate them.

Like any story of good versus evil, managers have to engage with and conquer the "dark side" of social media in order to reap its benefits. The "dark side" refers specifically to its risks and challenges. It is becoming increasingly difficult, if not impossible, to separate employees' personal lives from their professional ones. It is an area that requires careful management and will be covered here in detail.

All business problems are really "people" problems in disguise. For example, a "security problem" can occur when employees find ways to circumvent security policies or when hackers hack into a company's systems. The dark side of social media is not a primarily technical problem, but rather an issue of people needing to know how to apply the rules. In any organization, how rules or policies are written and how they are applied are two completely different things (commonly called unwritten rules and the law of unintended consequences). This is the reason why a clear social media policy must not only be in place, but why there needs to be a transparent relationship of trust between management and employees.

● ● ● ● ●

4.2 **The Overlap of Personal and Professional Life**

THERE ARE MAJOR DIFFERENCES between personal social media networks like Facebook and MySpace, and professional ones like LinkedIn and Ecademy. However, the distinctions between personal and professional social media networks are becoming less clear. Facebook, for example, expanded its platforms three years ago

SocialMediainBusiness.com

to include the business domain. Social media networks tend to imply personal use. However, since everyone is connected to and through these networks, companies should recognize the benefits of also being linked in.

In a normal business, however, it is inevitable for the boundary defining business functions to overlap the personal domain. Employees may think it is acceptable to browse sites like gambling sites, dating sites, and adult entertainment sites at work. These activities can, however, prove to be embarrassing to employers if social media policies are not in place to handle them. For example, is it acceptable to browse shopping, religious, or music sites during an employee's break time? If someone is working late, would it be permissible at that time?

To varying degrees, managers have to engage and deal with the impact blurred boundaries have on company operations by formulating a carefully thought out social media plan. A company must be absolutely clear about what is and is not acceptable during working hours on company equipment and premises. Having a plan in place that clearly outlines expectations and responsibilities is mutually beneficial to both the company and its employees.

FIGURE 25 · *The Overlap of Professional and Personal Lives*

> **"** *Our societies are increasingly structured around bipolar opposition between the Net and the self.* **"**
> (Castells, 2000, p3)

As mentioned above, the overlapped area between personal and professional social networks is proving to be a significant issue. Banning and restricting personal social networks in the workplace may not be an effective measure, as many networks are accessible from privately owned mobile devices such as smartphones, iPads, and tablets. Attempting to ban and restrict social media may even be counter-productive, as Skype or MSN Messenger, for example, is considered an essential tool for employees collaborating over long distances.

FIGURE 26 • *The Smartphone and Mobile Devices*

Senior management and key employees who are alienated from this new phenomenon will fail to become aware of any potential benefits that it could afford. Before the Internet was commonly used, fear sent companies into a panic that led to Internet use being banned in the workplace. Not all members of senior management within a company will be comfortable with the idea of the use of social networks. Even if they were open-minded about the idea, they may still not believe that its use has any advantages for the business. However, in time, they will come to see that no company can remain competitive without a social networking policy. Even if platforms like Facebook are banned in a workplace, it is still prudent to have a policy that stipulates how employees are allowed to use it to reference the company in their own time, using their personal devices (see Figure 27). Would a company that is completely against the use of social media in any form also ban employees from using their personal devices within the entire building? People will find ways to do these things regardless of company policy. A balanced policy is the best approach to deal with the intrusion of personal social networking into the workspace.

FIGURE 27 • *Social Media Breaks*

Many social networks first began as a tool for entertainment. Facebook, for example, has a variety of games available for users to play. Managers may, therefore, have the mistaken notion that social media is only for use during one's leisure time. Trying to explain how LinkedIn facilitates business connections would be as difficult as trying to explain the sixth sense. You might explain that you cannot get the same sort of interaction by walking into a room of business contacts or from mailing lists. However, for senior managers who still use a Filofax to list business contacts or collect business cards at networking meetings, it will take some time to adjust to the idea of using an online method for the same purpose.

● ● ● ● ●

4.3 Top Five Challenges from an Organization's Perspective

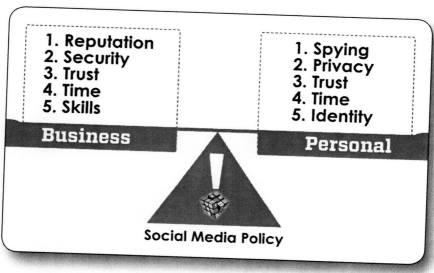

FIGURE 28 • *Top Five Risks and Challenges*

THERE ARE MANY REASONS WHY a company may decide not to use social networks within the workplace. Risks or challenges that organizations think are inherent to social media can sometimes be an insurmountable barrier. In the survey mentioned in Chapter 2, participants felt that the biggest risk organizations faced were all considerations of reputation. Below is a sample of responses the survey collected regarding concerns from a company's perspective:

4.3.1 Reputation Management

Social media is seen as posing a risk to a company's reputation. There is a concern that it might generate negative publicity. This concern about protecting a company's reputation can be split into the following categories:

Control Issues

"Social networks could lead to all sorts of situations we are not ready to deal with yet... this is the main reason we have not gone down this route."

Legal Issues

"... The company being afraid of being sued."

Consider the precedent set by a Twitter case in 2011, in which South Tyneside Council in the UK forced Twitter, through the US courts, to hand over the identity of individuals behind five Twitter accounts that had allegedly been critical of council officials. This case raises a number of important issues:

1. The Council has a duty of care to protect its commercial interests and those of its employees against malicious accusations.

2. Companies and individuals can no longer say what they like about others without possible repercussions.

3. People who have their names mentioned on Twitter can go to the court in the USA to obtain the name of the person behind the tweet.

4. The law is lagging behind the Internet developments.

Network Issues

"How do we manage the network issues so the company's reputation is maintained or enhanced? And how can we give the employees the freedom [to use social media] without getting distracted?"

4.3.2 Security – Hacking, Spy-ware, Bugs...

There is a fear of confidential information being shared and remote access technologies enabling outsiders to access sensitive company information.

"We are trying – to a degree – to ignore the security aspects of what people share about the company. We don't quite know what to do with it. For example we found content on YouTube that should not be there (relating to the business brand). So we are handling it case by case for some of the things we are not so comfortable with because we do not have a stance (policy) at the moment."

AskSteve.co

" *You have almost no control.* **"**

In 2011, the Sony PlayStation network was offline for a number of weeks as a result of an attack by hackers, leading to the service being withdrawn and the network security having to be significantly upgraded. More than 70 million client credit card details were compromised, indicating that security is a big issue that does have to be considered seriously.

4.3.3 Engaging in Dialogue and Conversation

There is a fear that damaging or unpleasant conversations about a company can take place without the company being aware.

" *Staff is talking about your company and whether the company is engaged with that conversation or not, it is taking place. Some of those conversations are quite unpleasant…* **"**

" *This is the biggest issue the big brands face. They are being talked about, and generally speaking, they are not starting or engaging in those conversations.* **"**

" *You are forced to engage with it and acknowledge what is being said.* **"**

4.3.4 Trust as Part of the Culture

A certain level of trust within the organization is required and is indeed a prerequisite for employees' use of social media to be successful. This entails individuals being accountable and taking responsibility for their use of social networks. As mentioned in Chapter 1, effective mechanisms for resolving conflicts or managing undesirable incidents should be in place in the event that something goes wrong.

" *We have not provided as an organization too much opportunity for these kinds of forums or online dialogue because we don't know what to do with the information if it goes wrong.* **"**

4.3.5 Wasting Company Time

Social networks are seen as a huge waste of time due to its social nature and its abundance of games. Time spent on social media platforms that is not business related can be seen as a bad thing, regardless of the huge learning potential it may provide.

"Facebook is for playing games and socializing and is a waste of company time and is not seen as a serious business tool in our company."

"Time spent on personal stuff while at the office… or spent with the social network internally but not directly on business."

"One issue arising is that older managers are generally not on these networks while their children are! …management does not embrace play as a part of work, and maybe there are areas where that is a flawed assumption."

• • • • •

4.4 Top Five Challenges from Individuals' Perspectives

The interviewees also expressed concerns from individuals' perspectives:

4.4.1 Lack of Time

There is a concern that activities on social media networks can take up too much of the user's time.

"Facebook can be very addictive and it's easy to spend the whole morning on it… because I was addicted myself, I know the danger once you are already on it… that you have a number of contacts… it becomes a vicious circle; the more you are on it the more time you have to spend on it."

4.4.2 Company Spying and Permanent Storage of Web Activities

Recruiters are constantly spying on potential employees and their respective employers. Footprints in the snow – any web page you have ever visited is recorded on a server somewhere.

> *If Facebook becomes heavily monitored, I suppose then you could move to a network less known that is not monitored.*

> *The danger is that people are not allowed to be themselves and let their hair down in their private life.*

> *Imagine being reminded of something you did as a teenager when you are older and the Internet still having the pictures to prove it.*

4.4.3 Maintaining Privacy

Another major concern from an individual's perspective is a lack of privacy. Social media networks can reveal a lot about a person. People tend to reveal more online than they would in face-to-face interactions. Divulging certain things online can also be a risk to personal security. The concern about the lack of regulation, the requirement to know the limits of what can be posted online, and the need to know how to control privacy settings on any social media platform cannot be dismissed. However, one way to mitigate the issue of personal safety is to make sure not to disclose certain information on social networks that could jeopardize one's safety.

> *The issue is where to draw the line between personal life and organizational life. It is a personal site ultimately – when I go out clubbing or football for instance I am not representing my company.*

> *How far can the organization be involved in my life? E.g. what should I do when the boss wants to become a Facebook friend?*

SocialMediaInBusiness.com

"The Internet and the whole publishing environment that it promotes are forcing you to be 'whiter than white.' For instance, if you were ever an alcoholic, a part-time stripper or something like that and it gets into the mainstream it will be there forever. A bit like a criminal record, but it follows you."

"Tools can be used to check people out that come for interviews. One bugbear is being constantly approached by recruiters or consultants trying to sell you on something."

"I would rather have a lower profile – that's the main reason I avoid these networks."

4.4.4 Trust and Misrepresentation

There is a requirement for the individual and the company to use these sites responsibly and not to take them out of context.

"An example I'd give of friends that are swingers – a guy's wife runs a swingers site. This had an effect on her husband's career in an organization, as he was a senior manager, and this was seen as a problem in case the media got hold of the story."

Reputation is everything, and it is incredibly easy to lose by accident.

"The real danger is if you are linked with something that is not you."

4.4.5 Identity Management

Social media tools enable you to join up parts of your life that are otherwise segregated in the offline world. This can initiate a social debate about double standards and how open-minded we are. Is self-censorship required? Do we need privacy from the company?

"We all have different identities/roles within different groups. E.g. I might be a father of children, a family man, play football, a corporate man, and a spiritual healer. The difficulty with Google etc. is that it brings all these different identities together, which

AskSteve.co

133

may not be what you want. You cannot control what you may have to reveal, or the amount you are comfortable revealing, and you have to accept it for what it is."

"*The biggest problem is for individuals to think they can behave in different ways in different places and not be found out. Some views are best kept to yourself!*"

4.4.6 **The Impact on the Business**

In order to fully consider the impact new technologies might have on a business, organizational design strategies must be implemented.

However, this section is not intended to cover the subject of change management or organizational or workplace design because these huge subjects are beyond the scope of this book. Instead, it provides a guide to give you an understanding that the process involved in attaining the benefits outlined in Chapter 1 will affect your employees and every part of your business.

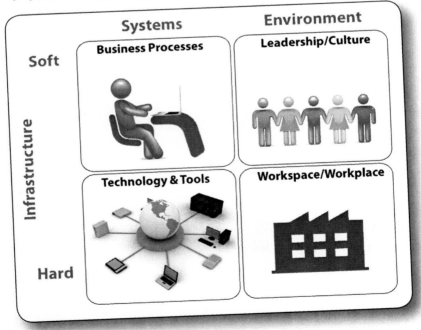

Figure 29 • The Importance of Visible and Invisible Impacts on a Business (inspired by Vangstad, 2002, p55)

Figure 29 can be described as follows:

The **hard infrastructure** is the part of an organization that is easy to measure and where there is typically a lot of data (information technology and tools, such as databases, networks, software, computers, printers, phones, etc.). The workplace and workspace, such as buildings, offices, furniture, and filing storage, are also part of the "hard" infrastructure.

● **Technology and Tools**

Organizational design must consider ways to efficiently implement two-way communication using social media tools. Access networks such as broadband and the distribution around the business needs to be adequate. The importance of the mobility of employees needs to also be taken into account. As you saw in Chapter 2, there are now innovative uses of smartphones, iPads, and tablet devices. Social media "apps" are now in the thousands. Many applications available on desktop computers are also now available on mobile devices. This is extremely useful and convenient for employees who need to be on the move. Twitter was one of the first applications to become famous for its mobility. It allows individuals to send quick short texts (no more than 140 characters) to let their followers know what they are doing in real time. Every major application accessible on desktop computers now has a mobile application that is downloadable for free.

Furthermore, simply having a computer connected to the Internet makes it possible for employees to work from home. Large companies can provide off-site employees with remote access to any files they might need from the company's network. A Virtual Private Network (VPN) in this case could provide security. A smaller company's security would be provided by security software, installed on all desktop computers and office laptops, and by the security features built into each software application in use. Technology works with businesses by providing the tools needed to enable staff to do their jobs effectively and efficiently.

The impact of security threats must not be underestimated. It is important to have a regular security review as part of your social media policy.

● **The Workplace and Workspace (Online and Offline)**

Organizational design can create additional meeting places like a lounge, coffee corner, or kitchen for informal communication to take place. Hot-desking can also be considered to promote flexibility in the workplace. It is also about designing online spaces such as social media sites in which employees can meet and relax in the same way possible in the offline environment. There is little consideration given to online spaces today. However, this will become increasingly important with the advent of holographic projection technology and augmented reality.

The key consideration here is opening a dialogue between the IT, human resources, and the property and facilities management departments. In many companies, these departments do not routinely meet to discuss the impact of social media on the organization. It is important, however, for these departments to communicate or collaborate more effectively using the combination of technology, the offline environment, and business processes to create more effective solutions.

Broadly speaking, the **soft infrastructure** is the "people" part of the business: the way they interact, share, collaborate, and communicate. These are the processes and culture of an organization that are largely invisible and are difficult to measure. Ironically, they are the biggest assets of most businesses. Social media helps with the visibility of these softer issues.

● **Business Processes (Change Management)**

The design of online and offline communication networks requires some con-sideration of the relationship among employees. It can incorporate communication processes, procedures to adhere to, and policies. Typically, as social media is introduced, ways can be found to improve business processes and, potentially, to design new services. The areas that are affected are:

1. Products and Services: researching and creating new products and services, product launch, customer support, and identifying new opportunities.

2. Customer Relationship Management: enhance the customer value proposition and improve customer selection, customer acquisition, and customer retention while growing the customer base.

3. Customer Social Responsibility: environment, health and safety, and community participation.

4. Operations Management: supply chain management, production, distribution, and risk management.

5. Improve Learning and Capabilities: people skills and knowledge.

6. Improve Information Technology: websites, social media, databases, and networks.

Remember, those who deliberate the role of social media in your organization will impact its implementation. Will it be an opportunity, a problem, or a strategy applied across the organization? The answer depends on decision-makers' understanding of the evolving social media and the company's information technology proficiency.

A company may choose to use the services of a web design firm as part of their social media strategy. However, these parties tend to approach social media from the point of view of technology rather than business, ignoring all-important business processes.

Therefore, it is important that all managers in your company have a good understanding of social media and the potential impact on your business. This is because it is management that creates a statement of intent for the general objective of the use of social media in the business. The policy needs to be drawn up with involvement of human resources, legal, marketing, and communications departments, and with input from the operational departments. The IT department provides the technology and tools, as required. The individual departments are then empowered to use social media opportunities and to create goals for their department or team.

In many companies, social networking is driven from the marketing and communications departments. This is especially true for business-to-consumer companies.

● Leadership and Culture

The leadership and the culture set the context in which social media will be operating in an organization. There are different leadership styles and varying cultures that will either be helpful or not when it comes to the implementation of social media initiatives. This is a reality that you as a manager have to work with and probably have little short-term influence to change. As part of the implementation of social media, the degree of transparency in decision-making, the values shared among employees, the unwritten rules, and formal and informal communication have to be considered. There is no doubt that social media can open the company up to a number of issues that were previously centrally controlled. Unofficial channels of communication can easily be opened up with both customers and employees on social networking platforms. It is therefore important to monitor and respond to what is being said about your company. It is also beneficial to be involved in these online forums as a contributor in order to direct the dialogue and ensure that all discussions stay within the boundaries your company sets.

All projects need to have support from the highest level of management in order to be successful. If the leadership at your company is supportive, it makes implementation a lot easier. One of the main barriers can be the general lack of understanding about what social media is or is not. It might be useful to cover this issue early in the communication process.

Organizational politics is something every company has difficulties dealing with due to its "people" element. The dynamics are constantly changing. One change of personnel at the executive level can have a major impact on the politics of the entire organization. Therefore, office politics cannot be underestimated. A savvy political operator will see social networks as something to be controlled or manipulated to their own benefit. Although office politics is prevalent in all organizations, senior management can be the last to know.

Organizational politics evolves as collaboration develops. Dilts and DeLozier (2000) categorized this under "sender and receiver" labels. The effect of organizational politics depends on who is sending a message to whom, the power relationship involved, and how freely views can be expressed. It is natural for an organization's management to want to manage an online social network. However, management's involvement in social media platforms may inhibit employees' natural openness. Online communication tends to be informal, but the knowledge that management may have access to anything shared online can change the nature of communication from informal to formal. After all, careers can be made or broken in bars and golf clubs.

Tapscott and Williams (2005, p46) said it best: "Rethink knowledge… knowledge is not something firms can possess. Treat it as something that emerges in relationships as people collaborate to achieve [an] objective." However, they added, "As networks take shape within and across enterprises, it becomes critical for organizations to develop a strategy to leverage knowledge across these networks and manage its exchange."

Organizational politics is a delicate issue that can have the effect of driving potential online communication offline. You might want to ask, what is the purpose of a particular social network and does it fulfill your requirements? It may be a case of establishing different networks for different purposes and allowing for multiple channels. Online networks such as Facebook do not yet possess the subtlety of offline networks and the ability to grade "friends" and contacts. Google+, on the other hand, has the ability to do this.

According to Bohm et al (1991), there are three basic conditions necessary for proper dialogue:

1. Participants must suspend their assumptions.

2. Participants must view each other as colleagues or peers.

3. In the early stages, there needs to be a facilitator who "holds the context" of dialogue.

These points are all relevant to company politics and management control of online networks in a real-life company situation. While many participants may enter into the spirit of things, there may be some individuals or groups who have their own hidden agendas. Policy-makers have an important role in acting as necessary facilitators but allowing enough rein for online social networking to flourish.

4.5 "Dark Side" Mitigation Strategies

GIVEN THE MANY RISKS AND CHALLENGES outlined in the previous section, it is tempting to pack up the idea of exploiting the benefits of social media for business. However, with your eyes focused on the prize, these risks and challenges can be confronted and mitigated.

Figure 30 • Five Mitigation Strategies

4.5.1 Consider Social Media as Part of Your Strategic Planning Process

Social media is now so pervasive that leaving its implementation to the IT department or the marketing department is not the best decision for most organizations. It touches most of your key business processes and impacts your business, as seen in Figure 29.

In order for the four elements of design to work, and for your organization to benefit from social media, they have to be considered together as a whole. It is generally regarded unwise to consider design-ing the offline workspace without considering the online workspace, the culture, and the business processes system. However, in the majority of organizations these functions reside in different departments with different agendas. It is therefore easy to fall into the habit of planning without having all the information needed.

Tapscott argues that an organization's design needs to encourage informal interactions:

"Genuine collaboration happens as much around the water cooler as it does in the boardroom. In the same way architects design shared interactive community spaces, digital environments need to offer collaborative content opportunities – both formal and informal."
(Tapscott and Williams, 2005, p6)

Ultimately, when attempting to implement social media use in the workplace, a forward-thinking manager must lay out a vision for the organization in which executives, management, and employees work together toward a common goal. Management must demonstrate that they are committed to open and transparent policies for organizational culture, so as to attract the best and most dynamic new employees. Transparency is a double-edged sword that can be moderated and controlled. At the same time, any effort to have transparency in an organization can be negatively affected by office politics. Putting in place policies for using social media at work ensures that it is not abused or manipulated in negative ways and that everyone benefits from its use.

4.5.2 Have Clear Social Media Policies

There has to be a clear policy to spell out acceptable behavior and procedures, given the degree of freedom social media platforms entrust to employees. Often, when new applications are introduced there can be some apprehension about perceived risks. Social media is "social" by its very nature, and to simply ban or restrict access is not a good strategy, given the potential benefits.

There also has to be a security policy in place in order to protect the company from possible external threats. This has to be carefully implemented to balance security with the limitless nature of social media. There has to be a forum where knowledge can be shared without worries and where dialogue can take place openly and responsibly.

The purpose of social media policy is to cover the risks and challenges outlined in this chapter:

● **Internal Social Media Policy** – informing your employees of acceptable behavior on social media sites.

● **External Social Media Policy** – planning exactly how your company will utilize social media to communicate with outside parties.

Social Media Policy – Suggested Content

● Consider compliance, communications rules, and governance.

● Hold employees accountable for anything written on social media sites.

● Remind that content posted must comply with the company's confidentiality and disclosure of proprietary data policies.

● Include a clause stressing that the use of social networking sites cannot interfere with an employee's primary job responsibilities.

● Review security policies and procedures.

● Allow employees a measure of privacy. The organization and its partners or affiliates can also not be referred to online without their express permission.

● Avoid encouraging referrals or endorsements, as even positive references can be misquoted by competitors and used against your organization.

● Make sure your social media policy sets out guidelines for managing crises.

● Clearly state what the grievance procedures are and ensure that they comply with your legal policies. Have your lawyers check that the policy is watertight.

● Ensure that legal issues such as copyright, plagiarism, libel, and defamation of character are also covered in your social media policy. Consult a legal expert on social media if need be, and include a clause in your policy document that holds employees responsible for reading the Terms of Service Agreement of the sites they use.

- Ensure that security reviews are conducted on a regular basis while minimizing the risk posed by the current security threats.

In drawing up a social media policy, all the key players in your organization need to be consulted. Personal standards will invariably set the tone for social media policies. However, since personal ethics and viewpoints can vary widely among upper management, your organization must establish one uniform guideline that will become the company policy. This needs to reflect the organizational culture and business procedures, not just how to interact on Facebook.

It is also prudent to issue a reminder to employees of the public nature of statements written online, as they may have unintended consequences. These statements will be visible to business competitors and recruiters, who may use them for their own purposes. If social networking users identify themselves as employees of the organization, your policies need to require that any personal blogs and other personal posts contain disclaimers that make it clear that the opinions expressed are solely those of the author and do not represent the views of the organization.

A good policy sets the boundaries and sets limits so that it protects and empowers employees. In these days of outsourcing and use of temporary workers and other partnerships, boundaries can be difficult sometimes to establish. Matters such as who is inside and outside the company need to be clearly established as a policy is drawn up.

Clearly, a certain amount of responsibility is placed on employees and individuals. They have a duty to protect their employer's confidential information and reputation. Due to the ease of access and reach of online networks, it can be easy to broadcast information that may not be appropriate.

In summary, all policy documents need to clearly require employees to think before writing a statement and to reiterate that employees will be held accountable and responsible for their online actions. Spelling this out in fine print is necessary to avoid any embarrassment.

AskSteve.co

4.5.3 **Tools**

**For access to examples of social media policies,
go to the online resources page:
www.SocialMediaInBusiness.com/Tools**

4.5.4 **Training and Development**

Skills-development training sessions can be arranged for both managers and employees. They can also be organized to foster a culture change in embracing social media. It is also worthwhile to train employees on the company's social media policy about conduct online and what is and is not acceptable in order to avoid any disputes and negative publicity.

A pilot project, or trial, is a good training vehicle. It is useful, real, and provides actual hands-on experience with the tools in question. It also provides hard data that an organization can use to examine possible effects of any changes in business processes. The organization can also use this data to compare the results of the pilot trial with the processes already in place, making it possible to choose the best option moving forward.

It is also often useful to have employees who are already enthusiastic about social media train other employees in both formal and informal environments. This could be done regardless of which department the individual is a part of. In every company there is a depth of experience that often goes untapped because the person may not be in the "right" department.

In order to prepare for unwelcome consequences of social media use, it is best to get everyone involved in training in order to make them aware of any issues. It can be useful to run worst-case scenarios to prepare employees for the unexpected, which is of course a paradox because you cannot prepare for the unexpected! However, training scenarios that force people to deal with unexpected events help to hone the ability of the team members to think on their feet when dealing with such events. A lot can be learned from these exercises.

SocialMediaInBusiness.com

4.5.5 Mindset and Culture

Social networks are linked with corporate culture. It is rightly argued that the culture of an organization, and by implication relationships between stakeholders, has many variables that come together to form a picture of the company as a whole. The picture of a company's informal communication must be one in which the use of technology is combined with face-to-face meetings. Online and offline networking need to work together; neither one can replace the other.

> ❝An organization's culture develops over time, and is slow to change, and is reinforced by the practice of people recruiting others whom they like. The informal organization, by contrast is quick to grow and transmute according to changing circumstances and the interaction of individuals within the organization.❞
> (Waldstrøm, 2003)

In the face of challenges from social media and other emerging technologies, managers and employees have to be ready, as these tools are here to stay. Management must foster trust among employees: trust to share knowledge, trust to be responsible online to protect the company's reputation, and trust enough to allow individuals some privacy.

For social media to benefit your organization, you must foster a business culture that is open, transparent, and conducive to flexible working and dealing with gray areas. Encourage managers who can develop better decision-making skills and are able to balance conflicting objectives, rather than blindly tick boxes. Most problems arising in the business environment involve balancing conflicting goals and paradoxical ideas, such as the team versus the individual, conforming to the rules versus breaking the rules, short versus long term, and investment in capital goods versus operational costs. Good leaders instinctively know how to analyze tomorrow's issues today.

Culture is a difficult area to change and can take a long time. Mindset, on the other hand, is easier to influence through a reward system designed to elicit the desired behavior. Rewards are a good tool in the hands of a good manager and, combined with the principles of trust, can be a powerful combination in both directions.

4.5.6 Fostering a Relationship of Trust

One of the opportunities of social media mentioned in Chapter 1 is the opportunity to enhance informal communication. A relationship in which employees and management trust each other helps mitigate the dark side of social media.

It is worthwhile to reiterate that informal communication cuts across formalities, making the processes within companies more efficient. Unfortunately, due to its spontaneous nature it can be more difficult to manage, control, police, or measure. However, there are plenty of tools that can help enhance informal communication from which to choose.

Online social media networks provide some of these tools. It is important to note that social media use does not advocate *spying*. This has been misconstrued as one function of social media that does interest certain types of managers. Such managers may see an opportunity to spy on employees, on their communication, and on the contacts they maintain. There is already strong evidence of employers vetting job applicants, for example, by examining the nature of their contacts and personal activities on Facebook and other network entries (Crail, 2007). Spying was actually one of the fears raised by some of the participants of the survey. This is not to be lightly dismissed, given the history of email and Internet vetting (Crail, 2007) and monitoring in the past. It may also leave employers open to legal charges of discrimination. There is, of course, the view in many organizations that individual employees using Facebook, LinkedIn, and other external platforms during working hours are wasting company time. Trust would come into play here, in that management would trust that their employees are actually using social media platforms to the benefit of the company.

It is also possible to take the view of the Trades Union Council that:

" *Facebook is just another way of using the web to organize your social lives... [Employees] have a right to a personal life and provided they do not breach reasonable conduct guidelines, employers should respect this.* "

(TUC, 2007, pp1–2)

Trust is a two-way street. This is a key issue that runs to the heart of the matter of online conduct.

Covey (2006) talks about the key determinants of relationships based on trust:

Your Character:

● Talking Straight

● Demonstrating Respect

● Creating Transparency

● Righting Wrongs

● Showing Loyalty

Flowing From Your Behavior:

● Delivering Results

● Getting Better

● Confronting Reality

● Clarifying Expectations

● Practicing Accountability

● Listening First

● Keeping Commitments

● Extending Trust

"Trust is the Glue of Life" Stephen Covey

In the context of online relationships, this list provides a good framework to work with – for a manager with employees, customers, and suppliers. One thing a lot of managers instinctively know is that trust takes longer to build than it does to destroy. Employees are watching for you to demonstrate that you walk the talk. If you do not, you will quickly be found out and you will probably be the last to know.

● ● ● ● ●

AskSteve.co

4.6
Take Away Points

• • • • •

- Organizations have to understand that social media is not IT. The technical risks and challenges highlighted by its IT function have already been mitigated to a large extent by the availability of user-friendly social media platforms, such as Facebook, YouTube, and Twitter. However, security is an issue for all, not just IT.

- Social media, like any technical application, is only a part of all that occurs in any organization. Thus, it has to be looked at in the broader context. Managers need to take into account the issues that arise from change management, such as effects on employees, processes, technology application, networks, and the workplace. It must be engaged with a holistic approach within broader Internet marketing strategies.

- There are some rather delicate issues that need to be managed and balanced between the individual and the organization. The top five risks and challenges from an organization's perspectives:

  - Reputation management
  - Security – hacking, spy-ware, bugs etc.
  - Engaging in dialogue and conversation
  - Trust as part of the culture
  - Wasting company time

- Top five risks and challenges from individuals' perspectives:

  - Lack of time
  - Company spying and permanent storage of online conduct
  - Maintaining privacy
  - Trust and misrepresentation
  - Identity management

- These challenges can be actively mitigated by having clear social media policies in place, training new and existing staff, and fostering a culture that is based on trust and is conducive to the change required. It is also beneficial to design the workplace, its processes, and informal communication to get the best out of employees.

CHAPTER 5

• • • • •

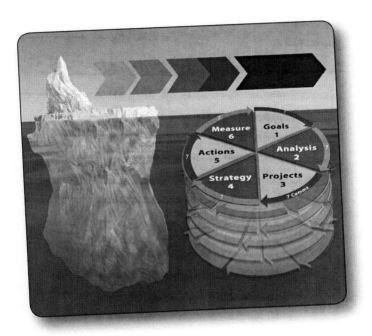

The

3-CORE

Project Success System

5.1 **Introduction**

PREVIOUS CHAPTERS PRESENTED THE FOUR KEY business opportunities offered by social media, discussed the evolution of the social media industry, looked at specific business applications and tools, examined the potential risks involved, and analyzed ways to mitigate them. This chapter will guide you in how to implement social media in order to achieve your aims in the most cost-effective and timely manner.

This chapter is written for planning and implementing social media applications in a small to medium size business or for a department within a larger business. The principle for larger businesses is the same, but implementation is more challenging due to the complexity of the internal and external environments inherent in large entities. Bigger companies may need to involve multiple departments, which would require additional levels of communication and coordination. This also often necessitates the use of customized applications, enhanced security, and enterprise-level software.

When implementing social media in your organization, it is beneficial to start with a relatively small pilot project as a test run. This will allow you to clearly measure its benefits and may also allow you to address any fears if your business environment is not optimal. Finally, the results of pilot trials also provide factual data that can then be used to justify undertaking the project on a larger scale and to create a project process for use on other projects.

This chapter also presents a framework for managing any social media project: The 3-CORE Project Success System. This consists of three elements: the core guiding process of the Project Development Cycle, the normal Project Stages, and the context of the Business Environment.

The Project Development Cycle is the key interactive process that is used to guide the manager prior to and throughout the project; it is the central blueprint of the implementation of the project. It is an iterative process that goes through many escalating cycles as the project develops through the stages, always having reference to the changing Business Environment.

SocialMediainBusiness.com

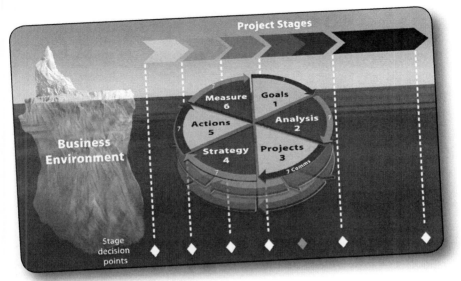

FIGURE 31 • *The 3-CORE Project Success System*

The Project Development Cycle is discussed in depth in Chapter 6, together with a case study of its application in Chapter 7. The current chapter focuses on the impact of the Business Environment in Part 1 and discusses the Project Stages in Part 2.

PART 1 – BUSINESS ENVIRONMENT

The Business Environment is the context in which your project has to work and the conditions necessary for successful implementation. For example, do your employees have the necessary skill levels, or is there a common language in your organization to discuss social media and provide a common context to start a meaningful dialogue? The one thing you do want to avoid is jargon and fancy language that divides people. As the manager, your role is to help everyone gain a clear understanding of what social media means to your organization. In this way, you can have full participation of people who do not know that much about the subject but know a lot about their jobs and probably know a lot more about social media than they are aware.

AskSteve.co

PART 2 – PROJECT STAGES

These are the time frames that structure the progression of a project. They are Briefing, Defining, Planning, Implementing, and Roll-out; each with clear outcomes. The importance of using pilot trials must be stressed in order to reduce risk, develop experience, and realize value. You can define or use your existing project stages.

• • • • •

5.2 **Part 1 – Business Environment**

ANY ORGANIZATION PLANNING TO BEGIN using social media or to initiate any other change project has to be aware of the many visible and invisible constraints that can get in the way of achieving a successful outcome. The foundations for the project must be strong and based on the needs of the business. For larger projects, it is often the invisible constraints within the organization that can be the most influential. A suitable analogy is that of an iceberg, where a large proportion of the issues awaiting you are hidden from view.

- No Management Support
- Conflicting Goals
- No Clear Outcomes
- Skill Gaps
- Limited Resources
- Department Silos
- Language Barrier
- No Business Case

FIGURE 32 • *The Business Environment: Pitfalls and Constraints*

Projects are rarely started from a blank slate. There are usually existing conditions and constraints that make each project unique and may require different approaches to meet each need. For example, a company may have a strict security policy that bans access to a social media tool such as Facebook. Another constraint managers may have to deal with might be the lack of skills and vision in the organization. There may be similar initiatives going on in the organization that need to be considered in your project planning process. The broader industry environment can also affect your project, and this needs to be considered. Two useful tools are the PEST analysis (Political, Economic, Social, and Technological) for the broader industry and a SWOT analysis (Strengths, Weaknesses, Opportunities, and Threats) for internal and external use.

In each of these cases, other managers may need to be persuaded to change company policy before any attempt at implementing social media can begin. In persuading management to undertake any change project, it is important to create a compelling business case and to be able to measure the return on investment (ROI).

Once the major obstacles and issues have been identified, the project initiator needs to ask the following questions to establish the initial boundaries for the project and to define its scope and areas of work. The following list is by no means all-encompassing, but it provides a good starting point.

- Is there a clear outcome defined for the project?
- Does the intention of the project support the business strategy?
- Is this the right project at the right time for my organization?
- What support is there from key players for the outcome?
- Do I have the remit to deliver the desired outcome?
- Who is going to manage the project?
- Are there other goals and projects that could conflict with this project?
- Are there any detractors to the project?
- Are there obstacles to different departments working together?
- Does my organization have the team and resources to complete the project?

- Are there language barriers that inhibit discussion of the project?

- Do pockets of experts dominate the conversation in key disciplines?

- If necessary, are there any customers prepared to participate in pilot trials?

- Can I gain access to the information I need?

- Do I have sufficient support at the senior management level?

- Does the project pose any significant risks to the organization?

When thinking of additional issues that may need to be addressed, questions that ask why, what, who, how, where, and when can be very useful.

Gaining an understanding of these issues is probably best done in an informal way before the project is formalized. This will enable the manager to get a feel for the kind of project scope, budget, and intention that is likely to be supported within the current organizational environment. For example, if there are a lot of potential obstacles and not that much support among the key players, then it is best to start small and set limited ambitions for the project. On the other hand, if there is great enthusiasm and support, it may be feasible to plan for a more ambitious project.

Training or briefing may be needed before you get started to create a common language for the project team and the stakeholders. The aim is to create an inclusive environment and more level playing field for those who may not be as familiar with social media as the other members of the project team; enabling everyone to contribute their unique experience, in a meaningful way, to the project. The most experienced technical people may not be the most experienced business people, and we need a blend of all the right skills for the project to be a success.

5.2.1 **Project Pitfalls to Avoid**

There are many reasons projects do not succeed. Some of the main ones are:

Pitfalls	Solutions
1. Lack of top management support.	Find a project sponsor with the appropriate authority and time to allocate to the project before starting.
2. No clear goals.	Create clear goals using the Project Development Cycle; define and refine them.
3. Lack of a business justification.	Create a business case as part of the project definition; get the project sponsor to sign off on it.
4. Nobody is taking responsibility for managing the project (especially if it goes off track).	Appoint someone appropriately skilled to manage the project.
5. Risks not identified or not managed.	Manage risk throughout the project as part of the project management process.
6. Unclear roles and responsibilities, wrong people in wrong roles.	Create a "roles responsibility matrix" and clearly allocate roles and responsibilities associated with work packages.
7. Scope management not properly managed, leading to scope creep.	Manage the change process as part of the project management process.
8. Lack of communication.	Create a communications plan.
9. Lack of appropriate skills.	Identify skills gaps and take action.
10. Lack of planning and management controls.	Hold progress meetings regularly to make sure you are on track, to manage progress, and to adjust the strategy as required.

TABLE 4 • *Project Pitfalls and Solutions*
. . . .

To download a SWOT & PEST Analysis,

go to the online resources page:

www.SocialMediaInBusiness.com/Tools

5.3 **Part 2 – Project Stages**

THE RATIONALE FOR UNDERTAKING A PROJECT in a series of phased stages is to provide a means of addressing any organizational constraints and obtaining buy-in from reluctant stakeholders. A decision point is created at the beginning and end of each stage. This also reduces project risk by generating appropriate justification and providing learning opportunities before moving forward to the next stage. The Project Development Cycle is continuously iterated throughout the stages as a method for planning and managing your projects, as you will see in Chapter 6.

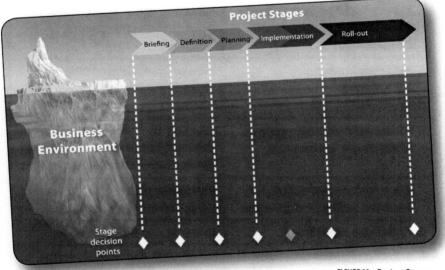

FIGURE 33 • *Project Stages*

The above diagram sets out the different planning stages that can be utilized over the course of the implementation of a project. These stages are especially important in organizations where there is a need to get the necessary organizational acceptance (buy-in) in order to allow a new project to proceed. It has to be stated that many companies or industries have their own stages (or phases), and you would be well-served by continuing to use those that are familiar to your staff and adapt the Project Development Cycle to your stages. The stage labels used here are for illustration purposes; the system is flexible and can be adapted to your situation. For smaller projects, some of the stages can be combined. For example, briefing and definition can be one stage, if the scale is small.

5.3.1 Briefing Stage

The briefing stage is typically the informal stage where you develop the project brief and establish organizational context that informs the intention and scope of the project. This stage often highlights areas of risk that need further consideration and research before the project can be properly scoped out. Suggested content for the written brief is as follows:

Goal	Detail a summary of the project, including desired goals.
Analysis	Provide, for example, the reasons for the project, any constraints, potential risks, and training requirements.
Projects	If multiple pilot trials are underway, identify each of these specific projects and the participants involved in each one.
Strategy	State the scope of the project and outline the business case; include the budget and timeline.
Actions	Outline the steps necessary to complete the Briefing Stage of your project.
Measures	Spell out the business justification in undertaking this project.
Communication	State how the project team will communicate with the identified stakeholders.

The Briefing Stage Outcome is a written project brief that you can use to develop the next stage, Project Definition.

5.3.2 Project Definition Stage

This stage is where you work with key players in your organization to formally define and establish the project and commit the resources needed to succeed. Depending

AskSteve.co

on the complexity of the project, it may take two to three turns through the Project Development Cycle, each one generating more details to complete the initial plan and business case.

To avoid wasting too much time getting into the details of the project, it is always advisable to have a quick overview (no more than a couple of hours) of the Project Development Cycle with the project team. This initial meeting is part of a discovery process that will enable team members to obtain a much higher understanding of the project requirements.

The thinking that underscores this section is that it is far better to get started with the work and not get too bogged down with justification before any work has been done. It can often take longer to justify a project than to do a simple "proof of concept" pilot trial that will provide far more useful information. It is necessary to have a plan, but it does not have to be an end in itself or to be overly complex.

Executive Summary	Overview of the document, a preview of the project.
Background	Reason for the project, any obvious constraints, and proposed solutions.
Intention of the Project	The project's goals and how they support the business strategy.
Scope	What work is included in the project, and what is not included.
Strategy	How the work is broken down into areas of tasks and key milestones.
Project Organization	Roles, responsibilities, and communication plans.
Project Management	How the project is going to be managed, including time, cost, and quality assurance.
Risks and Assumptions	A preview of possible risks and critical assumptions.
Project Budgets	Cost estimates for work packages.
Project Justification	Return on investment appraisal, once the budget is established.

The steps of the Project Development Cycle are designed to help you achieve a balanced approach between planning and implementation. The project definition is used to justify further funding and resourcing the project.

You will notice that the suggested content for written documents about your project follows a similar pattern; all the documents are, after all, about a single body of work. At the Project Definition Stage and then the Project Planning Stage, the content of the document simply gets more and more detailed. Any useful documents you prepare will have the following major topics, in the order of the table on page 158.

The Project Definition Stage Outcome is a document that can then be used in planning the project, which is the next stage.

At this stage you also need to identify the potential Project Manager and the Project Implementation Team.

Project Manager

It is essential that any social media initiatives have an appropriately trained, professionally qualified project manager to manage the project in a systematic way. I recommend the method of implementation in Chapters 5 and 6 because it is very easy to learn and not overly bureaucratic. This uses The 3-CORE Project Success System of the Business Environment, Project Stages, and the Project Development Cycle to manage the project.

There are more complex project approaches used by professional project managers involving large, complex programs of work (e.g. in the construction, oil and gas, and IT industries). My personal experience working as a professional project manager in the construction and telecoms/IT sectors is that these methods work well in these environments because there is already a supportive culture and mindset. Project management is also usually a senior level role in these organizations, with a lot of autonomy. This is rarely the case in industries where formal project management processes are not used. New projects are often allocated to a non-professionally qualified project manager whose day job is not project management, and who often lacks the authority required to undertake the task.

When adopted in organizations where project management is not part of the culture, these complex approaches can cause problems. They usually become overly bureaucratic, especially for small to medium size projects, unless a professional project manager with a lot of experience modifies them to ensure accountability is paramount. Large organizations and governments tend to favor complex project management methods, and this can spell the death knell for the small to medium sized project. This must be avoided if at all possible.

Project Implementation Team

Having established where you are and where you aiming to go, you need to appoint a team to run a pilot project in your environment. Also, you need to identify the stakeholders to be consulted as part of your communication plan. Appoint a senior management champion to sponsor the project and ensure senior management support. Also, appoint a project manager with the necessary skills, training, credibility, authority, and seniority within the organization to manage the project effectively.

5.3.3 Project Planning Stage

This stage builds on the Project Definition Stage, using the Project Development Cycle to provide a more detailed, actionable project plan. At this stage, a project team is established and the initial budget is allocated to develop the project plan. The suggested content for the project planning document is much the same as that detailed earlier for the project description, with the exception that significantly more detailed consideration is given for the specific work to be undertaken in such areas as pilot trials, communications, decision-making, and the like.

5.3.3.1 Benefits of a Pilot Trial Approach

The purpose of pilot trials in this context is to try out social media in a controlled, low-risk manner in your real-world environment. A pilot trial approach is useful as it enables you to understand the likely effects on your organization and customers. It is also useful to help in determining the larger project's benefits and resource implications, and to see the larger project as a microcosm of the real full-scale deployment. It is important to choose a pilot that is representative of the business and that will allow you to learn what a full-scale project will look like, as well as to identify scaling issues. You can often learn more from a well-designed pilot trial than from doing weeks of theoretical analysis.

The pilot trial not only tests the technology being used, but it also allows an organization to assess customers' reactions, as well as the business case and the impact on the organization. These are often over looked. It also enables project team members to acquire new skills and on-the-job training. Pilot trials can provide a host of additional benefits:

- Valuable team learning and on-the-job training.
- An opportunity to create a common language across the company.
- A number of "test" customers to provide input and feedback on all aspects of the project.
- A path for identifying any resource gaps.
- An avenue for identifying any research knowledge gaps.
- An opportunity for team building.
- Opportunities to obtain buy-in from senior managers.
- Reduction of risks.
- Justification to get the actual project started.
- Input for a full-scale business case.
- Rationale and justification for further projects.

An example of a pilot trial might be to try out an application (such as webinar training) in an internal setting before testing it with distributors and customers or deploying it on a wider scale. Innovative distributors and customers may be most likely to help you identify lessons to be learned, thus helping you to make any necessary adjustments before adopting the change completely within the organization.

Bear in mind the old saying in project management: "Don't grow the problem!" In other words, try to iron out as many issues as possible in the smaller trial in order to lessen the number of potential problems you may encounter if you deploy on a wider scale. Scalability is often an issue with social media and IT related projects,

AskSteve.co

and specialist experience may be needed from an experienced project manager to assess some of those common issues. Problems which arise after a project has been deployed on a wide scale will not be easy to deal with and can typically cost a great deal more to solve than if they had been dealt with in a pilot trial. This underlines the importance of the trial to identify issues before they create bigger problems. Also, do not expect everything to work the first time around. Overly optimistic planning is one of the main reasons for high support time and unnecessary costs.

Hidden issues within the pilot trial	X	Number of locations to which the issue has spread	=	Increased cost to solve

TABLE 5 • *Increasing Cost of Hidden Issues*

The Project Planning Stage Outcome is the completed project plan, including the business case and pilot trial, authorized by the project sponsor.

5.3.4 **Project Implementation Stage**

FIGURE 34 • *Real-World Implementation is a Vector*

After the Project Planning Stage is complete, it is then time to execute the plan. Implementation is not a precise art or science, and in the early stages of planning, frequent adjustments will be required. Imagine a boat at sea, sailing towards a destination (i.e. the goal) and having to make corrections to its course because of the wind and current, which are factors outside the control of the captain of the boat and the crew. In general, the more experienced the team, the less structure is required, and the more skilled they are, the better able they are to handle unexpected issues. Specialists in a particular area may be required for short periods to assist in setting the correct operating framework and to prevent costly mistakes.

Areas of work that have to be taken care of by the project manager:

- Authorizing and allocating work packages to meet milestones.
- Solving project issues.
- Assessing progress.
- Reporting on progress.
- Reviewing completed work packages.
- Managing quality issues.
- Escalating exceptional project issues.
- Reviewing milestones.

The Project Implementation Stage Outcome is a completed project in agreed-upon phases based on the project plan. You are now ready to move on to a wider deployment.

5.3.5 Project Roll-out Stage

This stage is typically outlined in the early stages of the project and is dependent on the allowable ambition of the project, based on the perceived risks and constraints imposed by your organization. It needs to be reviewed toward the end of the pilot trial.

The steps required in rolling out a project on a large scale are the same as the steps needed during the pilot trial. The only difference may be that instead of testing it on a handful of willing participants, all customers and other invested parties will now

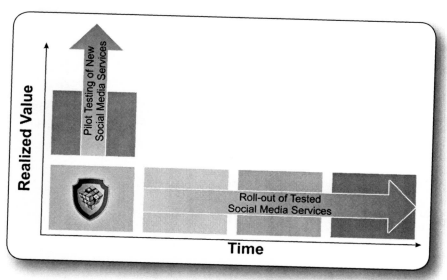

FIGURE 35 • *Roll-out Stage*

be given access to it. In other words, managers will only need to expand the access to the project that they have successfully brought through the testing phase.

For instance, an organization may use the Project Development Cycle to test-drive the use of GoToWebinar in its business processes. This would involve testing it with a limited number of customers and distributors. If the pilot trial was successful, you could then embark on a full-scale deployment, having learned from this experience.

In another example, consider an organization wanting to add more applications to its social media network in order to expand the scope. They could start off with trying out the applications within specific departments. For instance, Gotomeeting could be used as a trial communications project. Additional applications like wikis could then be added for document sharing purposes. Upon the successful completion of the pilot trial, managers would then roll out the applications for use throughout the organization, preferably in phases to reduce risk and support issues.

The Roll-out Stage Outcome is the addition of more projects to expand the scope of the existing project.

• • • • •

5.4
Take Away Points

• • • • •

- The 3-CORE Project Success System is a framework for managing any social media project. It consists of three elements:

  - Business Environment: This is the context of your business and the conditions under which you could be implementing any social media project.

  - Project Stages: These are the normal stages used in nearly any context for implementing most projects.

  - Project Development Cycle: This is a new tool, introduced exclusively in this book, for the specific work that must be done in your environment to implement a project, using the normal stages of project implementation.

- As you define your social media goals and move toward their implementation in your organization, it is important to remember the broader organizational context in which social media will be used. This will ensure that your social media goals align with the broader business goals.

- Phase in your project in a series of stages to provide the means of addressing any organizational constraints and to obtain buy-in from reluctant stakeholders.

  - Project Briefing
  - Project Definition
  - Project Planning
  - Project Implementation
  - Project Roll-out

- In implementing social media in your organization, it is beneficial to start with a relatively small pilot project to use as a trial. This will allow you to clearly measure its benefits and may also allow you to address issues that arise. Use the Project Development Cycle, continuously iterated throughout the stages, as a method for planning and managing your projects.

AskSteve.co

CHAPTER 6

• • • • •

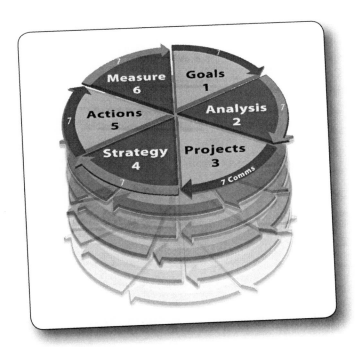

Project Development Cycle

AS WE SAW IN THE PREVIOUS CHAPTER, the Project Development Cycle is a continuous process to guide the manager and project team throughout all stages of the project, to take full account of the dynamically changing business environment, and to provide tracking and reference points at all times. The key thing to understand is that each cycle has to be completed with a time-out pause at the end, to enable the team to do some work between cycles and have some time for reflection. As you move through the project stages, you are continually building on the foundation of the information you have created in previous cycles.

The early project stages are related to planning the project and the latter are about implementing the project and project roll-out. Each stage has an output and decision point at the end of the stage to enable you to reach a decision that will set the stage for success in the next stage. The Project Development Cycle tasks reflect the project stages, i.e. initially they are about planning the project, and then they are used to manage and control the project as a change process.

One of the benefits of this approach lies in its simplicity. The process is also easy to learn and remember, especially for those who are not project managers as their main job. The time to learn this approach for an organization is much reduced compared to more complex processes that tend to be overly bureaucratic, take a long time to learn, and are less intuitive, especially for small and medium projects.

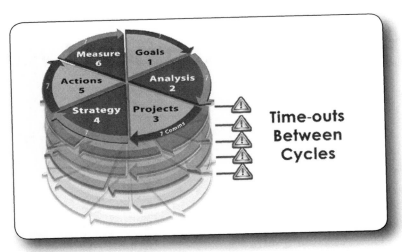

FIGURE 36 • *The Project Development Cycle*

6.1 **Goals**

IT IS IMPORTANT TO SET SOME GOALS to guide your activities in implementing social media. This is an iterative process that may change your goals, depending on the outcome of your analysis and the other steps of the Project Development Cycle. The purpose of this step is to answer the questions:

● What do we want to achieve?

● What value do we want to create?

● What are the key priorities for further analysis?

Dr. Stephen Covey (1999), author of *The 7 Habits of Highly Effective People*, says, "Start with the end in mind." Identifying your goals right from the start is the secret to a successful social media implementation program. Social media goals lie within the broader context of organizational goals and can be viewed in terms of a hierarchy, as illustrated in the diagram below.

FIGURE 37 ● *Goals Hierarchy*

SOCIAL MEDIA GOAL SETTING

A straightforward method of setting goals for a social media project within an organization is as follows:

1. Define a business goal.

It is important to create goals at the business level in order to give each project a direction. Brainstorming areas of the business that might benefit from social media support is one way to do this. Identifying these areas will allow you to set the goals that would be desirable. These need to be motivational, specific, measurable, and achievable within a well-defined time frame. Use your goals to create a strategic advantage for your business relative to your competitors and to create more value for your customers.

Typical Examples: Increase revenue by 20% within twelve months; increase profit by 10% within six months; increase market share in a specific niche by 5%.

2. Define a social media goal in the context of the business goal.

These are specific goals designed to support the achievement of your business goals. Building a social media presence for a new customer segment or a new product is one such example. You could also select a social media goal from the social media opportunities outlined in Chapter 1 to create projects. Here is a brief recap:

a. **Communication** – Use social media to enhance internal and external communications. For example, AT&T uses Facebook for customer service.

b. **Communities** – Use social media to gain access to an appropriate market (community) like LinkedIn.

c. **Collaboration** – Use social media to collaborate with colleagues across departments, similar to how Accenture uses its Knowledge Exchange.

d. **Collective Intelligence** – Use social media to access a bigger pool of ideas. For example, Starbucks uses My Starbucks Idea to achieve this.

Example: Increase profit by 10% within six months by accessing collective intelligence. Build a new web application for ideas, rolling it out first internally and then with customers once fully pilot-tested.

3. Refine the goals.

Refine your goals to have a clear, inspiring vision of the purpose of the social media program and the outcomes expected. Create clear and explicit principles and values rather than just rigid procedures.

Example of a new campaign: "Ideas Mean Prizes 10.6"

● Creating a campaign in stages, first internally and then externally, to find the best ideas to help us increase our profitability and improve our competitive position by at least 10%.

● The campaign could be know internally as "Ideas Mean Prizes 10.6," reflecting the internal goal of increasing profit by 10% over six months. The public campaign could be simply "Ideas Mean Prizes," reflecting the competition element.

Social media goals must support the achievement of business goals. The selection of the appropriate social media mix is a matter of judgement and experimentation to know what works within your organization and your target market. At the end of the goal-setting process, you need to have identified a specific social media project tied to one or more specific business goals. Social media initiatives and applications have to be carefully selected to support these goals. In addition, unless you have the necessary in-house expertise, it is worth considering hiring outside help or undertaking any necessary training, as this can save both time and money.

Throughout the project, the goals will be used to measure your progress and how much value you create for the business.

The next step is the analysis stage. This can have an impact on the goals you identify. For this reason, review your goals regularly as you cycle through the Project Development Cycle.

● ● ● ● ●

6.2 **Analysis**

SOCIAL MEDIA ANALYSIS MEANS getting the facts to enable you to make quality decisions and creating a baseline case of where you are right now. It is important to know your starting point, to enable you to measure progress towards the desired goals and to analyze the information gaps throughout the project.

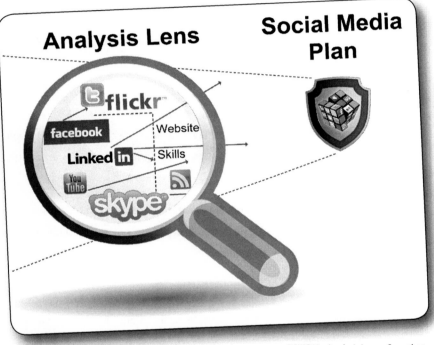

FIGURE 38 • *Analysis Lens – Snapshot*

Some questions to help guide your analysis step:

● What are your Strengths, Weaknesses, Opportunities, and Threats? (SWOT)

● What is the Political, Economic, Social, and Technical environment? (PEST)

● Who in your business is using social media and how effective are they?

● What applications are being routinely used and are there any restrictions?

● How does your website and micro sites compare to competitors in your sector?

- What is being said about your business and competitors in the social media?

- What is best practice in your sector? If there are no good examples within your industry, what are some of the best practices in the wider business field?

- How can your business use social media to achieve your business goals?

- How can you increase social media learning and knowledge across the company as a key capability?

- Which communities does your organization wish to engage, both internally and externally?

- Who are the stakeholders for the project?

This analysis is the key linkage to the Business Environment outlined in section 5.2. This could comprise doing an internal audit of your organization's existing infra-structure (e.g. websites, social media activities, skills, and capabilities), working out what is important to the business, and examining what your customers and competitors are doing. An audit can be conducted in a very short time. However, it could also take several days or weeks to complete, depending on the size and complexity of your organization and project.

When you initiate an audit of the social media applications that employees use, remember to assess all existing methods of informal communication within your business. It would be beneficial to collate the perceived benefits to employees, your clients, and stakeholders. Furthermore, explore the available social networks to assess those most suitable to your business (e.g. look at your existing intranets and other accepted networks).

Figure 38 shows that often organizations have existing knowledge spread through-out the company. Managers have to aim, however, to consolidate this scattered knowledge into a single meaningful picture of where the organization currently stands. Only then will you be able to decide on areas that require further research and what skills need to be externally resourced.

As part of the analysis, make sure you are collecting the information you need immediately as well as further down the road. The analysis requires changes, as

AskSteve.co

outlined in a later section, and connects the business environment throughout the project stages.

 To download an audit checklist and SWOT/PEST framework, go to the online resources page: www.SocialMediaInBusiness.com/Tools

● ● ● ● ●

6.3 **Projects**

The purpose of this step is to design your social media project, the areas of work, the products and services that it will deliver, and to identify the stakeholders. Once you have identified and refined your organizational goals and understood the business environment, you are ready to consider how social media can be used to help achieve these goals.

FIGURE 39 • *Social Media Project Design*

The method for creating high value projects:

1. Identify any available applications that support your organizational goals. It is important to understand the concept of what a product is and to remember that technology requires support when designing the products (see Figure 40).

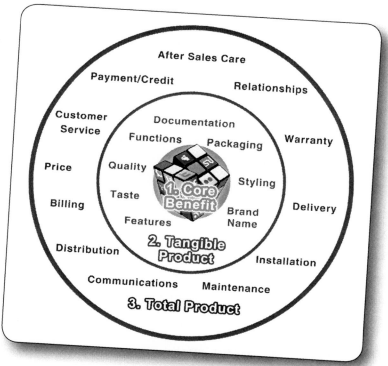

FIGURE 40 • *Three Levels of a Product*

An example of an organization at this stage of the Project Development Cycle is one that is ready to launch a new product and has distributors based in different parts of the world. Training the distributors on the features of the new product might involve the traditional approach of inviting everyone to a central location (e.g. headquarters), though this method is both time consuming and costly. The organization may decide, instead, to trial webinar technology, such as GoToWebinar.

It is understood that webinar technology is not necessarily a total substitute for face-to-face meetings. Human interaction is very important in most businesses,

AskSteve.co

but with the fast pace of today's business processes, it is useful to be able to have high-quality interim meetings. A social media site like GoToWebinar is useful to share information, such as product information, training materials, and training webinar recordings.

2. Identify how the application(s) would fit into the existing business environment and identify any potential constraints. During your analysis stage you will need to identify applications already being used, both within your organization and by your competitors. You will have a good idea about the context from the internal and external perspective of the organization. This provides the foundation for potential project scale, scope, and ambition.

3. Identify potential areas of work, e.g. what is in the project and what is not, in order to create the scope and broad areas of work to enable you to create a plan in the next step.

4. Identify a potential pilot project to trial the applications (see chapter 5.3.3.1 on the importance of pilot trials). You will then be ready to create a project based on one or more social media applications. Use Chapters 1–3 to help you generate some program ideas. When designing a social media project using more than one social media application, make sure you allow for these applications to work together, creating a unified approach.

5. Identify collaborators, stakeholders, and the resources needed to implement the project. Locate the appropriate resources and identify any training and skills gaps.

6. Once you have the project design, create a "product roadmap" of what exactly you are going to deliver and in what sequence. Ideally, a visual model or picture of the project has been created. This can be used to communicate what you are doing to other stakeholders, guide the roll-out program, and provide a baseline for reviewing through the Project Development Cycle.

At the end of this step, you need to have developed a social media design; identifying the application(s) and a potential pilot trial of the program. This will be refined with further iterations of the Project Development Cycle. Now, you will need a strategy to integrate this information into a unified plan, with key milestones needed to reach your goal.

For a checklist of questions and other considerations
to provide you with ideas, check the online resources page:
www.SocialMediaInBusiness.com/Tools

• • • • •

6.4 **Strategy**

THE PURPOSE OF THIS STEP in the Project Development Cycle is to create a plan that outlines the step-by-step milestones needed to achieve both the business and social media goals. Clearly, you will need to know the general direction in which you are heading. Try to avoid going enthusiastically in the wrong direction! Figure 41 below simply illustrates that the overall strategy is for each milestone to be influenced by the result of your analysis in order to guide your route to achieving your goal.

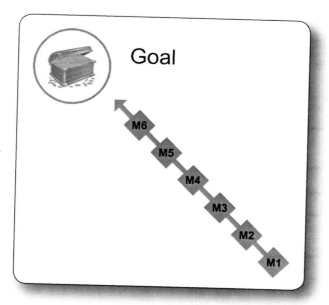

FIGURE 41 • *Social Media Strategy*

Doing the work described here will create an integrated social media plan. The social media strategy integrates business goals, project design, milestones, and actions into a unified whole. The plan assists you in organizing and allocating resources based on your organization's relative competences, constraints, and anticipated competitor moves.

Create clear goals and establish the pathways necessary to achieve them. This may require:

- Creation of "trial" customers (internal/external) to learn and understand how to create added value for them.

- Understanding the key issues facing your customers and opening a dialogue.

- Clarifying the industry value system and determining where your organization fits in.

- Understanding the value creation process for the organization.

- Understanding the importance of focus in achieving your goal.

- Determining if there are multiple pathways to the goal.

What are milestones?

A milestone is a package of work or stage of work that has to be delivered on a project. They are arranged in sequence along a "results path" towards a goal; on a more complex project there may be a number of logical results paths based on the outcomes for the project. It is critical to establish a starting point and end point for the project. It is also important to remember that on your way to the goal you have set, there will be intermediate points where you can measure progress, especially on a bigger project, or over a number of months where you need to measure progress over time. The intermediate points are the milestones (or work packages) that have to be delivered along the way to the goal. The milestones logically group together a number of actions; typically there would be less than 20 milestones on a project. These would be connected by dependency because you cannot proceed to the next milestone until you have completed the current one. For example, if building a house you would not start building the walls until you have completed the foundations.

Below are some suggested tasks to be considered as part of the social media plan:

- Integrate a plan for implementing social media projects across sites like Facebook, Twitter, YouTube, and LinkedIn.

- Select appropriate business project(s) to test out new approaches and to achieve some quick wins.

- Identify the stakeholders, resources, skills, and team members required to implement the project plan.

- Identify any risks and constraints.

- Provide a framework for effective implementation and management of the program and lay out actions for the next steps.

- Establish milestones to measure social media implementation and determine their effectiveness and impact on business objectives.

See Chapter 5 for suggested content of the project plan.

A plan is a "live" document that develops and grows throughout the project. An initial plan might be one or two pages. As you move through the Project Development Cycle, the plan develops in breadth and depth. If the plan gets too big, the tendency to read it reduces! It is best to keep it brief and focused on the desired outcomes.

An example of milestones based on the goal of creating an effective distributor communication program:

M1: Create a vision of the completed project.

M2: Establish the resources and budget for the project.

M3: Research the options to create the communications project.

M4: Choose the best options.

M5: Create the project plan, including timeline and business case.

M6: Create effective measures for the project.

The aim of this step is to create a social media strategy to support the broader objectives of your organization. It is a "live" social media plan that sets out the goals, resources, and specific project design, together with the milestones to be achieved. You will now need to translate this into specific, detailed actions in the next step.

For further explanation of milestones, go to the online resources page: www.SocialMediaInBusiness.com/Tools

● ● ● ● ●

6.5 **Actions**

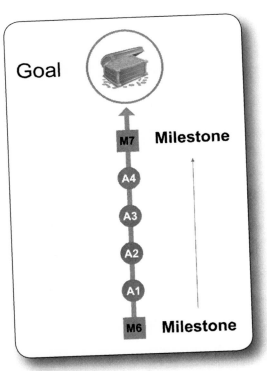

FIGURE 42 •

Actions to Achieve the Milestones

WHEN YOU HAVE IN PLACE A CLEAR GOAL, a baseline analysis, and a list of milestones, you need to consider what actions or tasks you must perform in order to achieve these milestones and succeed in your project. These can be reviewed throughout the project to measure progress.

Checklists can be helpful to create action plans. Actions have to be clearly associated with each specific milestone and be achievable. Using the example based on the goal of creating an effective distributor communication program, the "actions" step would look like this:

Strategy M1: Create a vision of the completed project

1. Plan a kick-off meeting to discuss the project.

2. Decide who needs to be present at the meeting.

3. Create an agenda based on the project stages and use of the Project Development Cycle.

4. Brainstorm the Cycle for one hour.

5. Allocate tasks to be completed by the next meeting.

6. Decide on the next meeting date.

7. Plan a 'check-in' procedure to occur prior to the next meeting to ensure participants are taking advantage of the time-out.

The outcome of this step is to create detailed tasks to be undertaken in order for each milestone to be achieved and to provide a method of reviewing progress.

● ● ● ● ●

6.6 **Measure**

THE PURPOSE OF THE MEASURE STEP is to provide a basis for assessing the effectiveness of your social media project and to enhance the whole Project Development Cycle process for future projects through continuous improvement.

It is critical to stress the importance of a well-known saying, "What cannot be measured cannot be improved upon." On the other hand, Albert Einstein said, "Not everything that can be measured counts and not everything that counts can be measured." Do not get stuck in analysis paralysis. An acid test is determining if you have fulfilled your business goals. In other words, it is judgement – a balance between what is important and having some way of telling if you are improving. For example, you may have a lot of visitors to your website or social media location, but if there is little interaction or if this does not translate into action, then you need to assess the effectiveness of your program.

There are three areas you want to measure on your project:

1. The Social Media

Social media projects can be measured at three levels: business goals, social media goals, and social media tactical data by means of measuring appropriate Key Performance Indicators (KPIs).

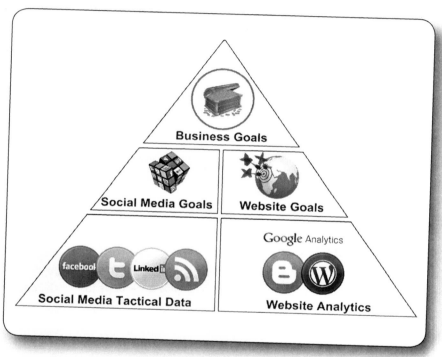

FIGURE 43 • *Measure – Social Media Aspect of the Project*

2. The Management of the Project

It is also important to measure the management of the project through the project stages. For this you can use the briefing document, the project definition document, the project plan, and one or more pilot trial. As part of these documents, the key tools are the timeline to measure and track progress against milestones, a budget to control cost, and the Project Development Cycle process to manage change.

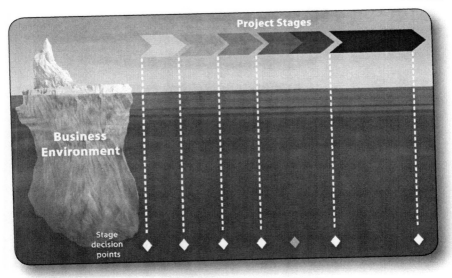

FIGURE 44 • *Project Stages and the Changing Business Environment*

3. The Changing Business Environment

The other area to measure is the changing internal business environment. Informal measurement can include looking at the levels of project collaboration between staff and comparing output to the amount of time taken. It can also include some informal post-project assessment, such as evaluating the sense of teamwork and any relationship improvements. We would only measure this on a larger project or where change was a central goal of implementing social media.

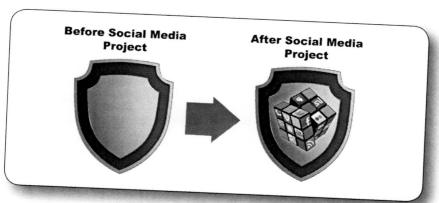

FIGURE 45 • *Before and After Analysis*

AskSteve.co

You may need to design a qualitative measurement system that is more meaningful, but may be more difficult to create. It might be as simple as having a "before and after" or a "with or without" social media comparative analysis, using some hard numbers to augment it. What was it like for your customers and your company before you implemented the new project, and what is it like after? You can also design projects that act as a comparison tool, especially if you have multiple branches; branch A with social media and branch B without social media. This would enable you to put a lot of otherwise meaningless data into context and create business information that can be shared and communicated within the organization, without the use of jargon that excludes participation from people unfamiliar with the terminology. There is a lot of new terminology in the social media world. It is worthwhile to repeat that, as you will need to create a common language within your organization to enable participation at all levels in the business and prevent excluding valuable experienced individuals, simply because they do not know the latest buzzwords.

The outcome of this step is to create the practical measures that will guide you and ensure that you are on track. The key here is to make sure you don't lose sight of the overall business goal.

● ● ● ● ●

6.7 **Communication**

THE PURPOSE OF COMMUNICATION as part of the Project Development Cycle is to set up the communication protocols between the project team and the project stakeholders. As described in Chapter 1, use of social media to enable communications is a major opportunity. Clearly defining the stakeholder groups and their information needs is an essential first step. *Think of it as ABC – Always Be Communicating.*

FIGURE 46 • *Communication – ABC – Always Be Communicating*

Communication is essential throughout the project for any chance of success. A key element is to provide information transparency and clear access to the project and the project team, both formally and informally. This needs to be specifically designed. Avoid titles such as "special project" or "special project team," as this immediately creates division, which is not what you are trying to do. The location of the team is also very important to ensure fluent communication and feedback. This is a two-way process between the project team and the relevant stakeholders. The importance of this cannot be overstated. Ensure there is a creation of a common language to facilitate dialogue, as previously stated.

The purpose of communicating social media benefits and getting feedback from employees and management is to demonstrate what is working and how it can benefit employees and the organization as a whole. This creates "buy-in" and allows for input to new projects as part of an ongoing change management process. Not everyone will immediately see the benefits of something that they may not understand. Some people might think that social media is purely marketing or an IT issue and really has nothing to do with them. However, social media impacts everyone within an organization; it might require different ways of working and, therefore, may necessitate changes to the workplace.

If your organization is in the early stages of adopting social media, then the emphasis needs to be more on creating the environment and mindset conducive to using social media. With experience, the importance of communication and its measurement becomes clear and is a vital aspect of determining the success of your social media project.

There must be a communication plan built into the overall project plan. This will set out the protocol for communication and feedback between the project team and the different stakeholders, both formally and informally. The communication occurs at two levels – project-based and broader organizational communication – and could consist of:

Project-based:
* Set communication goals and design for meaningful conversations.
* Develop a project communications strategy.
* Hold a project kick-off meeting with the sponsor.
* Decide how to handle changes to the scope and configuration of the product deliverables.
* Hold project progress meetings to review use of the Project Development Cycle.
* Support user group meetings.
* Stage decision points.

Broader-based Organizational Communication:

* Set communications goals for the broader organization on a larger project.

* Review the impact on the organization from a communication point of view, identified in Chapter 4 as Learning Curve, Training, Mindset, and Culture.

* Review the social media policy and anything that has been identified from your analysis work.

* Understand any training requirements.

* Remember the importance of information transparency: clear access to the project and the project team (both formally and informally). It is also important to communicate relevant meaningful information. A lack of information transparency is one of the key reasons a project may fail.

* Create a common language – for an organization to prevent the conversation being dominated by a few "experts," it is important to create a common language when we are dealing with something new. It is important for the project manager to demonstrate this by asking an expert to remove jargon, so we can all understand. The use of glossaries and common training programs, e.g. reading this book, will help to bring the team up to speed. As long as the whole organization has a common understanding about what social media means for the business, this will enable a broader input from more people with business skills rather than a few social media savvy people that may not have the appropriate strategic or operational experience.

* Use social media channels (e.g. blog, Facebook, Twitter) to communicate with your organization and stakeholders (anyone identified as part of the project communications plan). This also can be used as a training vehicle to create some quick wins.

* Communicate and build on quick wins, such as the outcome of pilot projects and small-scale trials.

* Recruit onto the project a number of people as catalysts or social media champions and seek to create a learning environment, through training, before you get started. It is important that the project team reflects and demonstrates what it is you are trying to convey to the wider organization. The mindset of the team is very important. Team members must be enthusiastic and understand the potential

benefits. In most organizations there are people with a lot of knowledge about social media, which is not necessarily gained in the organizational environment.

Examples of how you might capture feedback for your social media projects:

● Regular audits can be carried out to inform future programs, projects, and plans so that you know you are on track, based on what was agreed. You can figure out how well the social media policy is working in practice, recommend new projects, and understand the need for new skills and training across the organization.

● To get feedback from stakeholders, customers, and all those on the project, you can use question and answer campaigns, online polls, comments, structured feedback forms, and so on.

 To download a project review,
go to the online resources page:
www.SocialMediaInBusiness.com/Tools

∗ ● ● ● ●

6.8 **Time-outs – Importance of Time Intervals between Development Cycles**

IT IS VERY IMPORTANT TO ALLOW sufficient time intervals between major work cycles in order to gain a deeper understanding of the project requirements, time for reflection, and opportunities to gather additional information. Take the time to review and to do further research, rather than attempting to do everything in one go. Often, doing too much in one go is counterproductive and again allows the possibility of a "few good talkers" to dominate the process. You may end up going enthusiastically in the wrong direction.

This allows time for building a better, more coherent project team and for further analysis, such as:

- Completing any audits.

- Bringing in additional resources or skills.

- Talking to other departments about their plans.

- Researching the social media applications market in more detail.

- Obtaining pricing for specialist applications.

- Discovering the IT policies related to key applications.

- Getting training that the team and the stakeholders may need.

- Identifying other potential pilot projects.

- Reflecting on what was discussed.

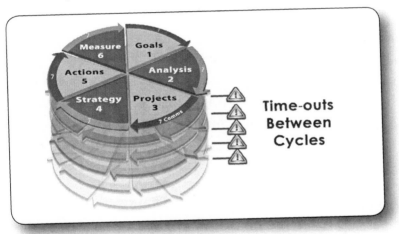

FIGURE 47 • *Importance of Time-outs*

In any case, it is necessary to complete each cycle in order to incorporate feedback and any lessons learned into the next iteration. In the planning process, managers need to not only examine the individual steps but also to always keep the bigger picture in mind. All the steps are interrelated; what changes is the depth and feedback you achieve over time, which in turn changes the overall plan. The key is not to get stuck on the individual steps and to focus on completing one cycle of the process each time.

Bear in mind the old saying in project management:

“I do not have time to plan but I have time to do everything twice!”

6.9
Take Away Points

● ● ● ● ●

- Using the Project Development Cycle for planning and implementing social media projects can enable an organization to achieve optimum social media implementation.

- It is an iterative learning process where each experience is used for the next cycle, with each turn of the wheel adding greater depth of insight. At the end of each turn on the cycle there will be a "product" of some sort and a decision point that will guide your work into the next Project Stage – or not. As explained in Chapter 5, the Business Environment of your organization and the work done in each Project Stage will interwork with the Project Development Cycle. If your Business Environment rebels against the product that results from a particular stage of the work, then a decision is likely to be made to discontinue the work until that disagreement can be worked out.

- Time gaps between planning cycles will allow for a deeper understanding of the project requirements, time for reflection, and time to gather additional information.

- Milestones are set along the path from where you are to the goal you want to achieve. They are extraordinarily useful in keeping you from going enthusiastically in the wrong direction!

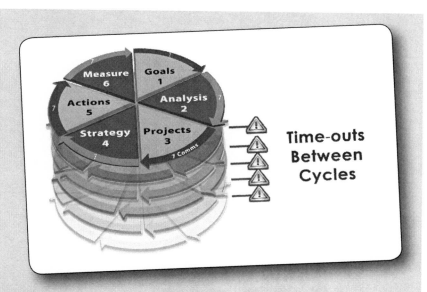

- **The steps of the Project Development Cycle are straightforward and logical, yet flexible enough to fit your organization's best way of doing business.**

  - Goals

  - Analysis

  - Projects

  - Strategy

  - Actions

  - Measure

  - Communication

CHAPTER 7

• • • • •

The Project Development Cycle in Action

CASE STUDY

UTHOR'S NOTE: The Project Development Cycle derives from 30 years of my work as a Business Project Manager and Consultant. I used the Cycle in the development, writing, and launch of this book and its related materials.

To help with understanding the Project Development Cycle in action, I will describe the process of launching this book. The reason I use this example is because most of the principles of implementing social media used here can be applied to the launch of any new project.

Steve Nicholls

● ● ● ● ●

7.1 Case Study: Book Project – THE BRIEFING STAGE

REMEMBER THAT IT IS IMPORTANT to plan a project in stages, as described in Chapter 5. Each stage requires <u>AT LEAST ONE TURN</u> through the Project Development Cycle and often a number of cycles, if the project is more complex. Think of the Briefing Stage as a brainstorming meeting where you have flip charts or perhaps even large pieces of paper taped to the wall of the room to write down ideas. Post-it notes are useful for recording ideas, as you can add, remove, or move them around as the brainstorming session develops.

What I am going to show you is an example of completing the first iteration of the Project Development Cycle at the Briefing Stage. This is a bird's-eye view of your project and need not take longer than a couple of hours to complete.

Goals

There were two main goals for this book project:

- To provide a solution to the overwhelming information managers have when it comes to social media by providing them with a simple framework.

- To fill this gap by writing a book that will guide managers through the social

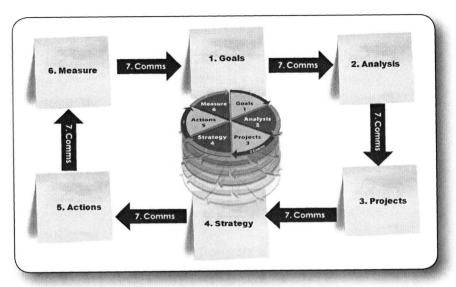

FIGURE 48 • *Post-it Project Development Cycle Meeting*

media implementation process. The implementation goal was to launch the *Social Media In Business* book by September 1, 2011.

Analysis

Use Internet sellers such as Amazon, Waterstones, and Barnes & Noble to investigate other available social media books in the professional field.

Project (Areas of Work and Product Design)

- Write the content of the book.

- Develop graphics for the book (the front and back covers and the content diagrams).

- Create a web presence (blog: www.SocialMediaInBusiness.com).

- Design the social media support needed to market the book.

- Create online courses based on the book.

Strategy

- Create milestones and timeline.

- Create a vision for the project.

- Identify resources required for the book.

- Decide on a publishing strategy.

- Write the book based on experience and MSc research.

- Locate an editor, graphic designer, and internal layout designer for the book.

- Create a web presence (blog: www.SocialMediaInBusiness.com).

- Design the social media support to market the book.

- For feedback, create an "ask campaign" for monthly Q&As.

- Create an online course (bookinar) based on the book, including a members' area.

Actions

Milestone 1 – Create milestones and timeline

- Project end goal.

- Project start.

- Brainstorming of key tasks.

- Re-arrange in logical sequence.

- Complete the initial tasks from the first Project Development Cycle and write up in the Briefing document.

Measure

At this stage, the measures identified for the project were:

- Track the number of books sold.

- Create a log for the number of people and questions received via the teleseminar campaign.

- Ensure website analytics (visits, page views, etc.) are collected (e.g. using the webhosting or implementing Google Analytics).

- Measure social media tactical data from each application (e.g. Facebook fans, Twitter followers, YouTube views of videos, E-zine articles stats, etc.)

- Create a teleseminar campaign to enable the author to connect with the reader on an ongoing basis. Answer questions arising from the book on a monthly basis and record these interactions.

* Tabulate interactions via blog comments, Facebook fan page community, and Twitter and LinkedIn Groups.

* Use all feedback for second edition and other products.

Communication

Set up a Facebook fan page and use my existing Twitter account, but remain low-key and focus on the writing of the book at this stage. Once the domain name has been selected, create a holding page to collect names and email addresses of people potentially interested in the book.

Having done all this work, I will have completed the first iteration of the Project Development Cycle at the Briefing stage. This is a bird's-eye view of my project that did not take longer than a couple of hours to complete.

AUTHOR'S NOTE: There are gaps in the work that reflect the unknowns or information that I did not have at that time. That is the purpose of additional Project Development Cycles – to pick up the missing information and to fill in the information gaps. The key is to always do a complete cycle each time and to keep thinking holistically, to avoid falling into the trap of silo thinking.

• • • • •

7.2 Case Study: Book Project – PROJECT DEFINITION STAGE

FOR THE PURPOSES OF THIS CASE STUDY, the outcome of the Briefing Stage, which is the briefing document, becomes the project definition document since it is a relatively simple project.

• • • • •

7.3 Case Study: Book Project – PROJECT PLANNING STAGE

AFTER A TIME GAP OF ONE WEEK to do some additional research, I had the core business case established for the book project. There were some gaps in the information I collected at the time. This is not unusual, as it is rare to have every single piece of required information at the beginning of projects. However, I was ready to start the planning stage by using the Project Development Cycle tool again.

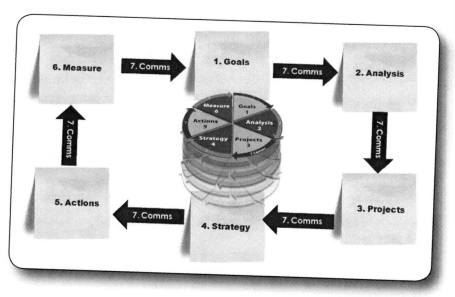

FIGURE 49 • *Second Project Development Cycle*

7.3.1 Goals

At the beginning of the second cycle of the Project Development Cycle I had a clearer vision for my book project, which served to inform my selection of a goal:

● Launch a credible social media book as a guide for managers in the business world by July 1, 2011, with the aim of selling over 5,000 copies. (This was delayed

SocialMediaInBusiness.com

by three months, as the original date was overly optimistic, having spoken to the editor and Amazon.)

- At this stage I selected a Rubik's cube to symbolize the millions of social media choices available for managers. The access to so many choices can make social media implementation something of a puzzle. (The Rubik's cube eventually became the image on the front cover and the symbol for my blog.)

FIGURE 50 • *Social Media Symbol*

- Create website to promote the book – SocialMediaInBusiness.com

- Create a series of articles to promote the book, leading up to the launch.

- Use the book content as the basis to create an online training course.

- Create tailored courses and consulting services for business-to-business marketing.

7.3.2 **Analysis**

AUTHOR'S NOTE: *As I am not part of a big company, the business environment is the* *broader market for business books, training, and consulting. The activities undertaken would be considered as the constraints if I were part of a medium/larger company. To simplify the analysis, I have not included my company's internal constraints.*

As part of the analysis for the book project I undertook the following:

● Searched Amazon.com and found many social media marketing books, mainly focused on marketing and technology. Decided there was a market for a book as a guide to help managers make sense of social media and provide a model for implementation.

● Talked to a group of managers to understand what they needed to know about social media and received a similar answer: what is it?

● Identified some groups on Facebook and LinkedIn, but did not find these very helpful, as most were coming at social media from a marketing perspective.

● Reviewed social media models via Google and decided to create my own model for Chapter 3 – Social Media Applications Guide because there was no dominant model for the social media applications market. There were some good ones, but too complex to fit on one sheet of paper.

● Used namechk.com to see if the name (socialmediainbusiness) was available on the popular social media sites.

I also discovered that my book idea was unique in that no other book provided an overview of social media in the business environment or provided a concise implementation guide for managers.

7.3.3 **Projects**

The main areas of work envisaged were:

1. Book content and design.

2. Web presence and design of social media support needed to market the book.

3. Online course based on the book.

4. Marketing plan for the book.

1. Book content and design

- Chapter headings.

- Plan for each chapter.

- Writing.

- Front and back covers – find graphic designer through my network.

- Diagrams for the book – additional work for the graphic designer.

- Bonus links to website in the text – create a table of contents and list of the resource part of the website. Provide added value items for download.

2. Web presence and design of social media support needed to market the book

- Create a book launch model (see Figure 51).

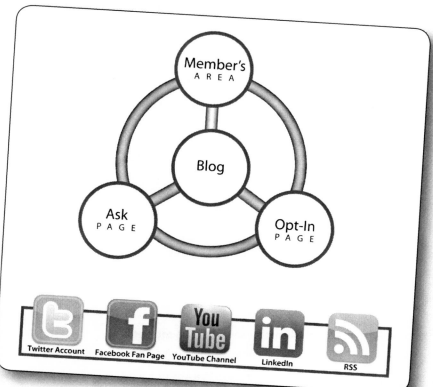

FIGURE 51 • *Book Launch Model*

● Blog: SocialMediaInBusiness.com

The blog is the main site for articles and comments.

- Create a diagram of electronic content for website and sales pages.

- Set up holding page to link to the list via AWeber form.

● Opt-In List Management

This is the entry point for new customers. They can submit their email addresses to be sent a summary of the book and to be given access to free monthly teleseminars.

- List management – Create autoresponder sequence – talk to my colleagues.

● Q&A Site

Prospective customers can ask a question about the book, and all questions answered are posted in the free section of the members area.

● Members area – See next section.

● Create a series of social media channels by using the following applications:

- Facebook fan page – www.facebook.com/SocialMediaInBusinessBook

- Twitter – Use Steve Nicholls' Twitter account or StrategyMindset; consider opening new account (at this stage I do not have to decide).

- LinkedIn – Update existing profile with details of the book.

- RSS – Create RSS button to make it easy to syndicate the content of the blog and easy for people to subscribe to updates.

- E-zine Articles – Create a series of articles based on social media issues raised in the book. Use Steve Nicholls' account.

- YouTube – Create channel for videos and webinars.

3. Create online and offline courses based on the book

- Presentation based on the book (30 min and 1 hour) – consider uploading to SlideShare once it has been tested with one of my clients.

- Create outline for the course based on the book.

- Consider an online project management course for managers who are not project managers as their day job.

- Create the outline for the fee-paying members area on the site.

- Create a group-coaching plan for managers who want additional assistance.

- Find pilot group of clients for the first course – set date.

- Find pilot client for in-house course.

4. Create marketing plan for the book

- Promotion of the book.

- Speaking engagements.

- Book reviews with professional institutions and magazines.

- Brainstorm other ideas.

7.3.4 Strategy

The milestones below (M1-M9) build on the milestones that were identified in the first turn of the Project Development Cycle.

M1 – Create a timeline and identify resources required for launching the book.

M2 – Create a vision for the project.

M3 – Write the book based on experience and my updated MSc research.

M4 – Create the book marketing plan.

M5 – Complete a web presence (blog: www.SocialMediaInBusiness.com).

M6 – Complete the social media support to market the book.

M7 – Develop an online course based on the book.

M8 – Launch the book.

M9 – For feedback, create an "ask campaign" for monthly Q&As.

7.3.5 Actions

These actionable steps build on the actions that were identified in the first iteration of the Project Development Cycle in order to reach the milestones for this project. Notice that more detail has been added here in the second iteration, and it is still not complete. Therefore, another cycle would eventually be needed.

M1 – CREATE A TIMELINE FOR LAUNCHING THE BOOK

MILESTONES	Month					
	1	2	3	4	5	6
M1 – Create a timeline and resourcing for the book	•••					
M2 – Create a vision for the project	•••					
M3 – Complete marketing plan for the book launch	•••					
M4 – Write the book	••••••••••••••••••••••••••••••••••					
M5 – Complete a web presence		•		••	•••••••••••••	
M6 – Complete the social media support to market the book		•		••	•••••••••••••	
M7 – Develop online course based on the book						••••••
M8 – Launch the published book						•
M9 – Create feedback – Ask campaign (monthly)						••••••

FIGURE 52 • *Timeline for Launching the Book*

- Identify resources for the book.

- Locate an editor towards the end of the main writing process.

- Identify a graphic designer for diagrams, book covers, and for the website.

- Identify a designer to lay out the interior of the book for publishing.

- Locate a proofreader to read the manuscript from the publisher before final approval for publishing.

- Use Skype for online meetings and Dropbox for file sharing, as social media collaboration tools.

- Use the Elance platform for working with the editor and managing files during the editing process; use Skype for online meetings (audio), both as social media collaboration tools.

Appoint an editor and graphic designer for the book:
- Create job specifications.

- Post on Elance.com and send to my personal network.

- Review the bids and draw up shortlist.

- Interview and get samples of work.

- Appoint them.

Appoint a graphic designer for the book:
- Find a graphic designer for illustrations and diagrams for the book. (Found via a colleague, located a designer based in the Philippines.)

Create budget forecast for the project.

M2 – CREATE A VISION FOR THE PROJECT

- Launch a credible social media book as a guide for managers in the business world.

- Create website to promote the book – SocialMediaInBusiness.com.

- Create resource website to provide enhanced features for the book (audio, graphics, table, html links, webinars, videos, and teleseminars). Keep the content up to date.

- Use the book to create online training courses and business consulting opportunities.

M3 – COMPLETE BOOK LAUNCH MARKETING PLAN

Choose a publishing and distribution strategy:
- To maintain editorial control and speed to market, publish book via Bookinars.co and distribute via Amazon.com.

- Select a strategy to get book into airport bookshops.

- Select a strategy to get book into corporate companies.

AskSteve.co

● Promotional strategy – to be decided.

● Pricing strategy – to be decided.

M4 – WRITE THE BOOK BASED ON EXPERIENCE AND MSC RESEARCH

● Decide on draft structure of the book and research schedule.

● Write one chapter per month.

● Create diagrams for each chapter and a chapter logo.

M5 – CREATE A WEB PRESENCE (BLOG: www.SocialMediaInBusiness.com)

● Locate web designer.

● Create Squeeze page – a page designed to collect email addresses of potential customers in return for a report or something of value.

● Create autoresponder sequence – a marketing tool to automatically send a sequence of emails out over a prescribed time frame or after a specific action (e.g. using AWeber).

● Design the web copy.

● Set up social media channels on the blog (e.g. YouTube).

M6 – DESIGN THE SOCIAL MEDIA SUPPORT TO MARKET THE BOOK

Create a model as set out in the Project Design – this is the framework for building the social media channels.

● Open Facebook fan page for the book and create vanity URL – after you have 25 likes on the page you have the option to change the website address (URL) to a shorter, more easy to remember version – www.facebook.com/SocialMediaInBusinessBook.

● Create YouTube channel.

- Use existing E-zine articles account for Steve Nicholls.

M7 – DESIGN ONLINE COURSE BASED ON THE BOOK

- Identify a client for piloting the courses.

- Design a bookinar based on the book, with four modules delivered, one per week.

- Consider creating a project management course for managers.

M8 – LAUNCH THE BOOK (DATE – TO BE DECIDED)

- Select launch date once I understand the full scope of the project and the resources identified.

M9 – FEEDBACK – CREATE AN ASK CAMPAIGN FOR MONTHLY Q&AS

- Set up ask campaign website.

- Set up the backend databases.

- Fix date for first monthly teleseminar to generate interest in the book.

7.3.6 Measure

I have now identified a more detailed set of measures for the project:

1. Actions for social media measures:
- Create Q&A site – AskSteve.co – as a forum for questions and answers in order to maintain dialogue with readers of the book.

- Create in-company workshop feedback forms – score and comments.

- Create open course training feedback forms – score and comments.

- Read and answer comments on the Facebook fan page wall, LinkedIn questions.

- Draft social media measures.

TABLE 6 – *Measures for the Book Launch*
. . . .

Level	Goal	Measure
1. Business Goal	Launch a new product to support consulting business	Value to the company – direct and indirect sales
2. Social Media Goals	Launch a Social Media In Business book	• Number of people taking the 'open' online training course • Number of organizations taking customized courses • Number of questions received via the AskSteve.co website and feedback provided about the content • Number of books sold – via Amazon. This converts into a monetary value
3. Social Media Applications	Website analytics	Use Google Analytics or access the hosting analytics for the blog, key pages, visits, and page views
	Blog	Age, audience, popularity, RSS feed subscribers, comments per post, etc.
	Facebook	Monthly active users, number of likes and dislikes, number of wall posts, number of visits per week, and advertising analytics
	Twitter	Total number of tweets, average tweets per day, followers, etc.
	YouTube	Views, comments, and subscribers to the channel
	E-zine articles	Number of views, URL clicks, click-through rates, comments, votes, ratings, most-viewed articles, profile views, subscribers, keyword stats

SocialMediaInBusiness.com

LinkedIn	Number of contacts in the network, number of questions answered
Customer list management – using autoresponder software (e.g. AWeber)	Number of new subscriptions per day, number of unsubscribed, total number on the list
Email campaign management	Emails sent, bounces, complaints, number opened, number of clicks, ad tracking, and revenue over time
Q&A (AskSteve.co)	Number of questions received, number of similar questions, word density and question spread

2. **Project measures:**

- Timeline

- Budget

- Meeting Schedule

- Stage Decision Point Reviews

7.3.7 Communication

- Identify the key stakeholders (i.e. my potential readers of the book).

- Create communication plan as part of the marketing plan. (In this project it is reasonably straightforward, so the communication forms part of the marketing plan. In a more complex project we would have to create a more comprehensive approach to communicating with the key stakeholders.)

- Low-key at the beginning of the project, until the book is written and the launch date is confirmed and fixed.

- Develop communication using social media channels once the book is "live."

• • • • •

7.4 **Case Study: Final Thoughts**

THE PURPOSE OF THE CASE STUDY was to get you thinking about the Project Development Cycle and how to adapt it to suit your needs. You will notice that there are still gaps, and these would be picked up on subsequent cycles through the project.

To see how I executed my book launch project, visit the Social Media In Business companion site and join the discussion! If you have purchased this book, you have access to the free part of the member area that has a lot of applications and tools for your use. There are also free resources available on the website.

www.SocialMediaInBusiness.com/Tools

• • • • •

CHAPTER 8

• • • • •

Next Steps

THE KEY QUESTIONS ARE where do you go from here and how do you move forward with your social media project?

● ● ● ● ●

8.1 How Do You Get Started with Social Media in Your Organization?

THE KEY STEPS to achieving a successful social media project are:

1. **Identify the business benefits for social media in your organization (Chapter 1)**

   As discussed in the previous section, the business benefits for undertaking a social media project must be clear. You need to identify what they are and why they are important to the business. It is also important to create a business basis for your project. Avoid jargon and a focus on tactical details (like fans, followers, and subscribers) as your primary means of justification. These may sound impressive, but it is better to focus on what they mean to the business in terms of revenue, market share, or growth rate.

2. **Use the applications guide to understand social media applications for your organization (Chapter 3)**

   As outlined in Chapter 2, understand why social media is the evolution of the Internet. Use the applications guide as a framework (Chapter 3) or choose one that works for your business and resonates with you. This will create a common language and framework to facilitate discussion and explore social media applications for your business, all of which can be used for training. More advanced detailed training would be provided, as required, by the pilot project.

3. **Recognize the social media risks for the organization and the employee (Chapter 4)**

   Be aware of the risks for your organization and review your social media policy on a regular basis (every 3–6 months). If you do not have a policy, create one – it need not be complicated (see Chapter 4).

4. **Identify the Business Environment constraints (Chapter 5)**

The business environment in every organization is different, and this is what makes every project different. The constraints, to a certain extent, shape the project, and this is the context in which the project has to fit. Changing business context can be challenging, especially if you do not have full management support. The key is to be aware of it and tailor the project approach to handle the risks.

5. **Use a staged approach to project planning to reduce risk (Chapter 5)**

The stages I outlined in the book are: Briefing, Definition, Planning, Implementation, and Roll-out. You can use your own stages if you like, and you can also combine or add additional stages if required.

6. **Use the Project Development Cycle to manage the project through the stages**

In addition to whatever stages of project development you prefer to use, a key element is to use a tool like the Project Development Cycle described in Chapter 6. It is easy for everyone in your organization to learn, and once they have used it a few times, it will become second nature. You will find additional benefits, because this process can be used to manage any project. Using the Project Development Cycle (Chapters 6–7) will also help to create a common language, which will enable your employees to have meaningful inclusive conversations about social media. Training programs and pilot projects will help foster a culture of experimentation and continuous learning and help the team understand the existing and emerging opportunities in a low-risk environment.

TO RECAP: THE 7 STEPS OF THE PROJECT DEVELOPMENT CYCLE:

* **Goals** – set goals in the early stages and review them throughout the project life cycle.

* **Analysis** – this step is mainly about working out where you are (your starting point) and what information you need throughout the project. It also keeps you in touch with the business environment.

* **Projects** – this is initially about identifying a pilot project and designing the social media applications to be used.

AskSteve.co

- **Strategy** – this is the step-by-step (milestone) plan; the major areas of work that are going to get you to your goal. This needs to be reviewed and updated regularly throughout the project.

- **Actions** – these are the individual tasks that you are undertaking to progress each step of your plan between milestones (strategy).

- **Measure** – the measures you set up initially and throughout the project are what you use to keep the project on track.

- **Communication** – remember your project ABC – Always Be Communicating. The importance of communication cannot be understated. Be transparent, be accessible, and most of all, be a model user of social media.

● ● ● ● ●

8.2 What are the Typical Obstacles that Prevent People from Getting Started?

THERE ARE A NUMBER OF KEY ISSUES that can make social media a difficult subject to deal with for organizations and managers. Most of these I covered in Chapter 4 – The Dark Side. The larger the project, the more important and influential these areas will become. The issues will never be far from the surface, and if not dealt with head on, will result in problems for the project and its execution. Some of the main issues are:

8.2.1 A Need for a Common Language

Google "what is social media" and you will be deluged with different and varied answers, even within the social media and Internet communities.

Any discussion about social media needs to be carefully framed, as you may be looking at it very narrowly: e.g. focusing on Facebook fan pages and Twitter rather than a more comprehensive, unified approach that looks at a strategy, not purely short-term tactical concerns.

There is a growing industry of "social media experts" with an inclination to focus solely on individual social media applications, such as Facebook and Twitter. Given that there are so many different classes of applications and each of these requires a huge learning curve to master, it is understandable that one might feel confused and overwhelmed. Without a frame of reference or blueprint, it can be very discouraging (Chapter 3 is designed to provide the framework for social media business applications).

Within your organization, it is equally important to develop a common language that everyone understands rather than having exclusive groups of "experts" leading the way. Remember the "paradox" that the best collective intelligence comes from lots of independent decisions aggregated together rather than just a few experts working as a team.

Everyone in your organization has to become proficient in the basics of social media and understand where they fit in so that they can contribute in a meaningful way. I believe that the ability to understand and utilize social media in an effective way will become a core building block of business in the future.

Remember the six blind men in the poem in the introduction. They all thought they were right, but they did not understand the whole of the elephant, just the bit they first experienced. In medium and large organizations, it is very easy to fall into this trap if we do not keep an open mind and have a common frame of reference. A common language is essential to enable meaningful conversations about social media within your organization. The ability to be proficient in the language of social media will become a prerequisite to doing business and creating a competitive resource.

8.2.2 Social Media is Not Just About Facebook, Twitter, YouTube, and LinkedIn

There is a common misconception that social media is simply another channel to market and is about putting up pretty Facebook, Twitter, or YouTube pages to attract fans, followers, and subscribers. These can be very useful marketing tools, but without an integrated strategy and a rationale, they will not do a whole lot for you – it is a very limited view of social media.

I hope from Chapters 1–3 you understand social media is a broad evolution of the Internet that is continuing to evolve, with many different applications and ways of using social media to benefit your organization. Applications that gain popularity have to have relevance and be useful to customers because the switching cost is so low. Facebook may or may not be the future, as we see with the demise of the popular MySpace of three years ago. The Facebook of three years ago is not the same Facebook of today: it has evolved with new applications and functionality.

8.2.3 Differing Mindsets and Perceptions

In most organizations people will be at different levels of understanding and starting points regarding social media; some at expert level, some just getting started, and some thinking it is just for kids and irrelevant to the business.

Some use it extensively in their private lives, while others use it hardly at all. These differences can also include demographic differences – typically, there can be a generational difference in attitude about the use of these tools and technologies. There has been a longstanding belief about social media that it is only for playing games and hanging out with friends and not a serious business tool. This perception is slowly changing, but do not underestimate the power of this mistaken belief if it goes unchallenged. As I have demonstrated, social media is not a panacea, but it is a very powerful business tool in the right hands.

8.2.4 Social Media is Not Free

The cost to you and your organization is time…lots of time! Social media has a steep learning curve and innovation is proceeding at a furious pace. It is important that you allocate time for your employees to become familiar with the basics so that they can see the opportunities and do not become out-of-touch. This is not an easy judgement to make, especially if those making the decisions do not fully understand the potential. Therefore, social media management briefings can be a useful tool to develop the conversation inside your organization and create common understanding.

8.2.5 Deal with the Security Issues

This is a real issue that needs to be handled as part of your social media policy and not used as a reason to avoid participation. If your senior management does not have sufficient strategic understanding of social media, then education, training, and briefing will be the first step.

What is becoming clear is that in future you will not have too much choice about participating in social media, because it is only a matter of time before your customers or competitors will force you to change, even if your organization resists. Banning key social media tools is futile because, as we discovered in Chapter 4, it is easily by-passed via the use of increasingly powerful mobile devices. In Chapter 4, I outlined how important it is to have a social media policy to handle social media conduct.

Your organization's readiness for change is a key consideration.

8.2.6 Visible and Invisible Impacts on the Business

Social media can affect far more of your business than you may be aware of and it could be coming in through the back door. The rise of mobile computing (smartphones and applications) and individual use of social media outside of work, such as Facebook, dating sites, YouTube, and gaming, are many of the ways this is happening.

The areas it may impact need to be reviewed over time. Currently, the most influenced are workplace and workspaces, technology and tools, leadership and culture, and business processes.

AskSteve.co

8.2.7 The Balance of Power Between Organization and Individual

From the survey I carried out, there are concerns with both the organization's and individual's perspectives about social media:

Organization	Individual
● Reputation	● Spying
● Security	● Privacy
● Trust	● Trust
● Time	● Time
● Skills	● Identity

The key to managing these is a good social media policy.

● ● ● ● ●

8.3 What are the Strategies that Overcome these Obstacles?

THE GOOD NEWS is that there are ways to manage the key issues that arise in your organization by:

● **Business planning** – make social media part of your business planning process.

● **Social media policy** – have one and enforce and update it regularly (including a security review).

● **Training programs** – use them to create a common language and understanding throughout your organization.

● **Mindset and culture** – this is a longer-term area to change and requires multiple efforts to make lasting changes.

● **Trust** – foster a relationship of trust, particularly in areas that are sensitive, such as privacy and security.

8.4 What is the First Step to Getting Started?

THE FIRST STEP IS TO START the briefing stage. Create a brief to define the potential program. Using the Project Development Cycle, this is typically completed informally to establish the organizational context, initial intention, and scope of the project. It will also highlight any risk and considerations for what pre-work might need to be carried out, such as training, briefing, and so on.

An example project brief:

Goals	Detail a summary of the project, including desired goals.
Analysis	Provide, for example, the reasons for the project, any constraints, potential risks, and training requirements.
Projects	If multiple pilot trials are underway, identify each of these specific projects and the participants involved in each one.
Strategy	State the scope of the project and outline the business case; include the budget and timeline.
Actions	Outline the steps necessary to complete the Briefing Stage of your project.
Measure	Spell out the business justification in undertaking this project.
Communication	Plan how the the project team will communicate with the identified stakeholders.

Once you have started the process of developing the brief, the next steps become much clearer. Continue to use The 3-CORE Project Success System as a guide to developing your projects with as many cycles as are necessary.

It is important to realize that there is a balance to be struck between planning and doing, and this comes with experience of using the system. The key is not to get too worried about getting everything perfect at the start. It is much more productive to get started, and in doing so, you improve and learn.

AskSteve.co

The 3-CORE Project Success System provides you with a low-risk framework to progress your project and build the necessary support as you go along. This way you can work gradually towards your end goal, however ambitious that may be, and develop the necessary business justification and allies as you go along.

Used wisely, The 3-CORE Project Success System is an excellent way of creating change, even in business environments that are not as supportive as they could be!

AND FINALLY...

Social media can be beneficial in terms of bringing people in an organization together into a community. The good news is that once you have implemented your first project, no matter how small, there is learning at many levels and it gets easier. People understand the process and also see the benefits. Social media can change your whole business and how you relate with your employees, customers, and suppliers. It can enable you to design new working spaces, both online and offline, and may force your industry and your business to change beyond all recognition.

Managed well, it can be a major strategic asset to your organization; it is not, however, a panacea; the rules of business still apply, and there is no substitute for common sense, focus, and good people. The good news is, no superhuman skills are required to master social media and anyone can learn it.

I hope this book has gone some way to raising your awareness and understanding of what social media is and and helping you understand effective ways of introducing it into your organization.

Thank you for spending your valuable time reading this book. I wish you all the success implementing social media, and please ask me the most burning question that arises for you after reading the book at:

www.AskSteve.co

I hope your question is one that I answer on my live Question and Answer sessions. So give it a try and tell me how you get on.

I hope our paths cross again and we meet in person.

Best wishes,

Steve Nicholls

References

Arthur, C and Fox, K (2011). *How the iPad Revolution Has Transformed Working Lives.* The Guardian. www.guardian.co.uk/technology/2011/mar/27/ipad-tablet-computer-users-rivals

Barreto, C (2009). *Cloud Computing Growth Predicted by Coda Research.* http://charltonb.typepad.com/weblog/2009/05/cloud-computing-growth-predicted-by-coda-research.html

Bohm, D, Factor, D, and Garrett, P (1991). *Dialogue – A Proposal.* www.david-bohm.net/dialogue/dialogue_proposal.html

Brown, R (1965). *Social Psychology.* New York: Free Press

Castells, M (2000). *The Rise of the Network Society* (2nd edition). Blackwell Publishing

Covey, S (1999). *The 7 Habits of Highly Effective People.* Simon & Schuster: Free Press

Covey, S (2006). *The Speed of Trust – The One Thing that Changes Everything.* Simon & Schuster: Free Press

Crail, M (2007). *Survey: Email, Internet and E-communications Policies.* IRS Employment Review, issue 881

Crampton, S, Hodge, J, and Mishra, J (2005). *The Informal Communication Network: Factors Influencing the Grapevine Activity.* International Personnel Management Association

Cross, R, Nohria, N, and Parker, A (2002). *Six Myths About Informal Networks – and How to Overcome Them.* MIT Sloan Management Review, pp67–75

Dilts, R and DeLozier, J (2000). *Encyclopaedia of Systemic NLP and NLP New Coding.* NLP University Press. www.nlpuniversitypress.com

eMarketer (2011). *Worldwide Social Network Ad Spending: 2011 Outlook.* Research and Markets. www.researchandmarkets.com/product/f686e6/worldwide_social_network_ad_spending_2011_outlook

SocialMediaInBusiness.com

Gapper, J (2008). *Wikipedia Is Popular but Scary*. Ft.com Business Blog.
http://blogs.ft.com/businessblog/2008/01/wikipedia-is-pohtml/

Gartner (2011). *Gartner Says Worldwide Mobile Device Sales to End Users Reached
1.6 Billion Units in 2010; Smartphone Sales Grew 72 Percent in 2010*. Gartner
Newsroom. www.gartner.com/it/page.jsp?id=1543014

Gens, F (2008). *IT Cloud Services Forecast-2008, 2012: A Key Driver of New Growth*.
IDC. http://blogs.idc.com/ie/?p=224

Goff, R (2011). *Location-Based Services: Foursquare vs. Facebook Places*. Social Media
Examiner. www.socialmediaexaminer.com/location-based-services-foursquare-vs-
facebook-places/

Hendrickson, M (2007). *Nine Ways to Build Your Own Social Network*.
http://techcrunch.com/2007/07/24/9-ways-to-build-your-own-social-network/

Hillis, S (2007). *Companies Shifting Virtual World Strategies*. Reuters.
http://secondlife.reuters.com/stories/2007/10/11/companies-shifting-virtual-
world-strategies/

Hoegg, R, Martignoni, R, Meckel, M, and Stanoevska-Slabeva, K (2006).
Overview of Business Models for Web 2.0 Communities. University of St. Gallen,
Institute of Media and Communication Management. www.alexandria.unisg.ch/
publications/31411

Holland, L and Ewalt, D (2006). *Making Real Money in Virtual Worlds. Forbes*.
www.forbes.com/2006/08/07/virtual-world-jobs_cx_de_0807virtualjobs.html

IDC (2011). *Worldwide Quarterly Mobile Phone Tracker*. www.idc.com

Inc.com, Inc. (2010). *Six Smart Business Uses for the iPad*. Business Insider.
www.businessinsider.com/six-smart-business-uses-for-the-ipad-2010-11

Internet World Stats (2010). *World Internet Users and Population Stats*.
www.internetworldstats.com/stats.htm

Janis, I (1983). *Groupthink: Psychological Studies of Policy Decisions and Fiascoes*.
New York: Houghton Mifflin

AskSteve.co

Jellinek, D (2011). *The Future of Reality is Augmented*. Edge.
http://edge2011.wordpress.com/2011/03/05/the-future-of-reality-is-augmented/

Kolbitsch, J and Maurer, H (2006). *The Transformation of the Web: How Emerging Communities Shape the Information We Consume*. Journal of Universal Computer Science, volume 12, no. 2, pp187–213

Krackhardt, D and Hanson, R (1993). *Informal Networks: The Company Behind the Chart*. Harvard Business Review, pp104–111

Lynch, C (2008). *Four Free Wikis Worth Trying Out*. CIO. www.cio.com/article/445813/Four_Free_Wikis_Worth_Trying_Out_

Marshall, D (2010). *Measuring the Growth of Cloud Computing*. VMblog.com.
http://vmblog.com/archive/2010/06/21/measuring-the-growth-of-cloud-computing.aspx

Mayfield, R (2003). *Social Capital of Blogspace*. http://radio.weblogs.com/0114726/2003/04/09.html

McAfee, Inc (2010). *Web 2.0 – A Complex Balancing Act*. McAfee, Inc
http://mcafee.com/us/resources/reports/rp-first-global-study-web-2.0-usage.pdf

Morton, S, Brookes, N, Smart, P, Backhouse, C and Burns, N (2003). *Managing the Informal Organization: Conceptual Model*. International Journal of Productivity and Performance Management, volume 53, no. 3, pp214–232

O'Reilly, T (2005). *What Is Web 2.0? – Design Patterns and Business Models for the Next Generation of Software*. http://oreilly.com/web2/archive/what-is-web-20.html

Reardon, M (2010). *Augmented Reality Comes to Mobile Phones*. CNET.
http://news.cnet.com/8301-30686_3-20017965-266.html

Reisinger, D (2011). *IDC: Apple iPad Secures 87 Percent Market Share*. CNET.
http://news.cnet.com/8301-13506_3-20028801-17.html

Spencer, S (2007). *SEO: Can Wikipedia Help Your Business?* Practical Ecommerce.
www.practicalecommerce.com/articles/413-SEO-Can-Wikipedia-Help-Your-Business

Surowiecki, J (2005). *The Wisdom of Crowds*. Random House

SocialMediaInBusiness.com

Tapscott, D, and Williams, A (2005). *Rethinking Information Technology and Competitive Advantage – Part II: Strategy in the Age of Collaboration.* New Paradigm

Tapscott, D, and Williams, A (2007). *Wikinomics – How Mass Collaboration Changes Everything.* Atlantic Books

TUC (2007). *Facing Up to Facebook.* TUC Briefing on Online Social Networking and Human Resources. www.tuc.org.uk/extras/facinguptofacebook.pdf

Vangstad, A (2002). *Strategic Internal Communications in Virtual Organizations.* Karlstad University, Sweden. www.vinco.se/pdf/nyheter/D-uppsats.pdf

Waldstrøm, C (2003). *Understanding Intra-Organizational Relations through Social Network Analysis.* Aarhus School of Business

Watts, D (2003). *Six Degrees – The Science of the Connected Age.* W.W. Norton & Co

Wray, R (2007). *Companies Look for Real Benefits from the Virtual World.* The Guardian. www.guardian.co.uk/technology/2007/jul/14/news.business

Yahya (2009). *The Benefits of Wikipedia.* http://yahya257.blogspot.com/2009/06/benefits-of-wikipedia.html

• • • • •

Further Reading

Go to the online resources page: **www.SocialMediaInBusiness.com/Tools**

A Range of Learning Opportunities is Available

Social Media In Business is a practical guide for incorporating social media into the workplace. All types of business professionals will gain insight and learn practical steps to implement social media strategies in their organizations.

To purchase *Social Media In Business*, go to www.amazon.com.

In addition to the book, readers will be able to supplement their learning experience with a range and variety of tools intended to inform, aid, and support their work to incorporate social media into the success of their organization.

- **Social Media Applications Guide** (www.SocialMediaInBusiness.com/Store)
  This guide is an electronic version of Social Media In Business: Chapter 3, plus additional tables of clickable links to specific social media applications.

- **Social Media In Business – Training** (www.SocialMediaInBusiness/Training)
  This Training Centre offers a range of resources and online training courses that develop the themes and details of the book. For example, "Social Media In Business Bookinar" is a modular online course that follows the book: expanding on its ideas, applying them to the real-life situations of participants, and facilitating discussions among participants and with Steve about unusual situations.

- **Question and Answers about the Book** (www.AskSteve.co)
  Connect with Steve on the Internet, where he will answer questions raised from issues in the book.

- **For additional information please see the online resources at:**
  www.SocialMediaInBusiness.com/Tools

About the Author

Steve Nicholls – BSc (Hons), MBA, MSc

Steve is a hands-on consultant, guiding strategy implementation in both large and small organizations within Europe, North America, and Asia.

Steve started out as a project manager in skyscraper construction. After his MBA at Henley Business School in 1992, he applied his project management expertise to grow businesses and new ventures in the communications and technology industries. Over the years, Steve has added millions of dollars of value to his clients' bottom line.

Steve has taught hundreds of people the secrets of effective project management and has implemented advanced Internet applications since the early 1990s with organizations such as: British Telecom, Ciena Corp., Deltathree, Inmarsat, John Laing, and the NSPCC (UK children's charity). Today, he continues to provide social media consultancy and project management training. Steve also holds a BSc (Hons) in Building Construction from Reading University and an MSc in Organisational Development and NLP (2008) from the University of Portsmouth Business School.

Web addresses:

www.SocialMediaInBusiness.com

www.AskSteve.co

Glossary

A

analytics Using statistics, research, or software to gather data which will help in the decision-making process. Google Analytics is a free online service for gathering website usage statistics.

application (app) Computer software or program enabling the user to perform a specific task or set of tasks. Applications can be for computers or mobile devices, including smartphones.

augmented reality The real world, experienced via a computer or device which 'augments' reality with computer-generated audio or graphics.

B

back-linking Inbound hyperlinks from one website or blog to another. Back-linking is important for search engine optimization.

blog A website or section of a website where an individual or group can share their thoughts and media, e.g. an opinion piece article, image, or video. Arranged in chronological order, with newer entries appearing first.

blogging platform A software application or online service that supports blogs. Examples include WordPress and Blogger.

bookinar An online seminar based on a book or paper, often used for remote learning.

business environment Conditions and constraints within an organization that affect how a particular project or policy is implemented.

C

cloud computing Internet-based network offering a shared pool of computing resources, including server space, applications, and data, which users can access remotely.

SocialMediaInBusiness.com

collective intelligence	A pool of independent thinkers, both inside and outside an organization, offering a wide variety of ideas and helping to guide decision-makers.
company spying	Spying on employees' online activity through monitoring social media or analyzing server records.
crowd smarts	*see* collective intelligence
crowdsourcing	Outsourcing tasks normally performed by an employee or contractor to an undefined, large number of people, or 'crowd.' Almost always achieved via the Internet.

E

e-commerce	The buying and selling of goods or services via the Internet.

H

hacking	Relating to security, hacking means digitally breaking into computers and networks; hackers may be motivated by profit, corporate spying, publicity, protest, or simply the challenge of circumventing network security.

I

identity management	Controlling different aspects of personal identity on the Internet; resolving conflicts and inconsistencies in an individual's online identity.
information brokers	Independent individual or business, usually with powerful connections in a specialized field, who researches and reports on specific information for clients.
instant messaging (IM)	Real-time text-based communication between two or more people, via computers or other digital devices. E.g. Yahoo! Instant Messenger or Windows Live Messenger.
intranet	Private computer network within an organization used for sharing information and resources.

AskSteve.co

K

keyword   On websites, keywords are specific words which relate to the content of a web page; helpful in search engine optimization.

L

location services   Software applications for web-enabled mobile devices which detect the location of the user and can provide location-specific information.

M

marketplace   A space, in the real world or online, where goods and services are bought and sold.

market intelligence   Analyzing a particular global market using economic and social statistics, such as demographics, population data, and total consumption levels.

market research   Surveys and polls to evaluate consumer reaction to a particular good or service; conducted through social media channels or traditional methods.

measurement   *see* analytics

media sharing   Sharing digital media, such as images, texts, videos, and slide presentations, between two or more people across different online platforms.

meta tag   A particular word or phrase used to tag a web page or article; helps search engines find relevant content.

microblog   Shorter than a blog; an online space where people share short comments and snippets of media. E.g. Twitter.

milestone   In project management, specific goals marking each step of the project development cycle.

mobile Internet   Web-enabled mobile digital devices, including iPhones, BlackBerrys, Android-based smartphones, iPads, and other tablet computers.

SocialMediaInBusiness.com

O

opt-in list

List of email addresses provided voluntarily by users; often used for distributing newsletters or updates.

organizational design

Designing the physical environment and management structure of an organization to maximize efficiency and performance.

P

pilot project

Small-scale test or trial of a project in order to identify potential problems or improvements before the main project gets underway.

plug-in

Software that enhances another piece of software or an Internet browser; usually application-specific and cannot be used independently.

project stages

The time frames and agreed outcomes that structure the progression of a project: Briefing, Definition, Planning, Implementation, and Roll-out.

Q

Quick Response Code (QR code)

A 2-dimensional barcode which can be read by QR readers and some mobile devices, including smartphones.

R

relationships mapping

Using social network analysis to map relationships between people, e.g. employees; helps managers understand how social networks are operating within the company.

remote training

Online or distance learning, via e.g. webinars, teleseminars, Bookinars.

reputation management

Improving the reputation of an individual or organization by attempting to remove negative feedback and highlight positive feedback, generally on the Internet.

AskSteve.co

resourcing	Providing the staff, funding, and other assets needed to successfully undertake a project.
RSS	"Really Simple Syndication": Standardized format for publishing frequently updated content on the web, e.g. blogs or news headlines.

S

search engine optimization	Helping search engines index and find a website or blog, mostly through incorporating specific keywords into the text.
Search Engine Visibility	How easily a website is found by users searching for related content; how high up the list it is displayed by search engines scanning for a particular search term.
smartphone	Mobile phone with computing and/or Internet facilities, e.g. iPhone, BlackBerry, or Android phone.
SMS	"Short Message Service": Text message sent between two or more people via a mobile phone.
social capital	The quality and quantity of connections within a social network.
social media	Web-based communication that is primarily for social interaction; highly interactive and user-generated, and may include the sharing of photos, music, videos, and polls.
social networking service (SNS)	A web-based platform for social media, allowing users to share content and to build relationships with other users and communities with similar interests. E.g. Facebook, Twitter, or the business-oriented service LinkedIn.
spyware	A small piece of software that can be installed (usually secretly) on computers to monitor the user's activity without their knowledge; often combatted with anti-spyware programs.

T

tablet	A mobile computer, somewhere between a laptop and a mobile phone in size and weight, which is usually operated

SocialMediaInBusiness.com

	by a sensitive touchscreen and on-screen keyboard. E.g. iPad or Samsung Galaxy Tab.
teleseminar	A training or information seminar which is attended by people in various distant locations, usually via teleconferencing or online tools.
time-outs	The time interval between development cycles in a project; used for reflecting on recent progress and gathering resources for future work.

V

viral growth	The "snowball effect" on the web; taking advantage of word-of-mouth marketing by spreading messages on the Internet.
virtual meetings	Conducting a meeting between two or more people in different locations, via the Internet.
virtual world	An online community, often part of a game, in which users interact with one another in real time via avatars. E.g. Second Life.
Visible Market Presence	Visibility of an organization within their industry, in both the global marketplace and local market niches.
Voice over Internet Protocol (VoIP)	Communication over the Internet, primarily using voice but these days also incorporating video and SMS. E.g. Skype.

W

Web 2.0	A new vision of the World Wide Web as a highly interactive, user-centered community where all users have the power to create, collaborate on, and share web-based media.
webcasting	Broadcasting over the Internet.
webinar	A training or information seminar conducted over the Internet.
widget	A small computer program that can be installed on a website or computer to deliver customized content.

AskSteve.co

Index

A

Accenture *61, 62, 170*

Active Worlds *108, 122*

advocacy sites *see* ideas platforms

Alexa rankings *69, 70*

Alterian *120, 121, 122*

Amazon *54, 77, 96, 116, 205, 208*

analytics *103, 121, 208*

Android *58, 72, 76*
    Market *101, 122*

app *see* applications

Apple *13, 43, 72, 77, 96, 101, 107, 122*
    iCloud *77*
    iPad *21, 58, 59, 73, 74, 126, 135*
    iPhone *58, 59, 72, 76*
    Store *101*

applications *13, 15, 16, 21, 22, 26, 28, 51, 55, 60, 63, 66, 73, 75, 77, 78, 84, 92, 93, 97, 99, 100, 101, 103, 105, 108, 112, 120, 122, 135, 141, 150, 164, 171, 172, 175, 176, 202, 210, 212, 215, 216, 217*

AskSteve.co *209, 220*

augmented reality *72, 74, 75, 88, 136*

B

back-linking *105*

Baidu *69, 71, 102*

Basecamp *78*

BBC iPlayer *79*

Blackberry *58, 72, 76*

Blogger *69, 71, 105*

blogs *30, 41, 42, 61, 69, 92, 96, 97, 100, 104, 105, 106, 122, 143, 187, 202, 203, 206, 208*

bookinars *82, 205*

Box.net *78*

Brainrack *119, 122*

broadcasting *21, 79, 92, 93, 98, 122*

bugs *16, 129, 148*

business

    environment *17, 21, 37, 145, 150, 151, 152, 159, 165, 168, 173, 174, 176, 183, 213*

    opportunities *12, 15, 16, 21, 22, 24, 26, 27, 28, 29, 50, 64, 66, 80, 81, 88, 92, 93, 100, 102, 108, 120, 122, 136, 137, 141, 146, 150, 156, 170, 188, 205, 212, 213, 217*

    processes *75, 112, 121, 136, 140, 141, 144, 164, 176, 217*

buying behavior *54*

C

campaigns *32, 40, 47, 50, 57, 97, 120, 121, 171, 188, 203, 207, 209*

Camtasia *97*

case studies *see* examples

change management *134, 136, 148, 186*

Cisco *32, 41, 42, 43*

civil uprising *13, 40*

cloud computing *76, 77, 78, 79, 94, 96*

Coca-Cola *13*

collaboration *15, 26, 28, 46, 47, 55, 57, 58, 59, 60, 61, 62, 63, 85, 89, 92, 108, 109, 110, 111, 112, 122, 138, 141, 170, 183, 204, 205*

    Accenture example *61*

    external *60*

    internal *59*

Collective Intellect *121, 122*

AskSteve.co

collective intelligence *15, 26, 28, 43, 52, 53, 54, 55, 56, 57, 58, 62, 92, 116, 122, 170, 171, 215*

Starbucks example *56*

communication *15, 21, 26, 28, 32, 35, 36, 37, 38, 39, 40, 41, 45, 46, 47, 53, 58, 59, 60, 61, 62, 74, 78, 80, 81, 85, 86, 89, 92, 93, 94, 95, 98, 99, 102, 106, 109, 110, 121, 122, 135, 136, 138, 139, 145, 146, 148, 150, 155, 158, 160, 170, 173, 179, 180, 184, 185, 186, 187, 209, 214*

Cisco example *41*

external *35, 36, 170*

formal *36, 37, 38, 80, 89, 138*

informal *32, 36, 37, 38, 39, 80, 81, 136, 138, 145, 146, 148, 173*

internal *35, 36, 37, 38, 53, 80, 81, 85, 87*

communities *15, 26, 28, 31, 42, 43, 44, 46, 49, 61, 63, 82, 88, 92, 100, 115, 122, 170, 173, 214*

LinkedIn example *49*

company spying *16, 132, 146, 148, 218*

conferencing *see* meetings & conferencing

ConnectMeQR *76*

consumer reviews *117*

content management *105, 121*

crowd-funding platforms *see* ideas platforms

crowd smarts *see* collective intelligence

crowdsourcing *55, 58*

culture *13, 15, 16, 22, 32, 35, 36, 37, 39, 40, 47, 59, 60, 64, 80, 87, 109, 130, 136, 138, 141, 143, 144, 145, 148, 159, 160, 186, 187, 213, 216, 217, 218*

D

dialogue *16, 37, 86, 87, 89, 130, 136, 138, 139, 142, 148, 151, 178, 185, 207*

discussion sites *92, 115, 116, 122, 202, 207*

DIY social networks *92, 108, 122*

DIY wiki platforms *92, 112, 113, 122*

Dropbox *63, 78, 96, 109, 204*

Dunbar's Law *49*

E

eBay *102, 122*

Ecademy *83, 85, 104, 122, 124*

e-commerce *101*

Elance *110, 122, 205*

email *33, 58, 76, 78, 95, 121, 206, 209*

Epinions *117, 122*

Essence of an Elephant *23, 24, 215*

Evernote *78, 101*

evolution of the Internet *15, 20, 66, 212, 216*

examples *17, 44, 55, 56, 78, 85, 95, 96, 98, 99, 101, 103, 105, 107, 110, 111, 113, 116, 118, 119, 120, 122, 170*

   collaboration (Accenture) *61*

   collective intelligence (Starbucks) *56*

   communication (Cisco) *41*

   communities (LinkedIn) *49*

   local & global (Groupon) *33*

E-zine *202, 207, 208*

F

Facebook *15, 21, 24, 26, 30, 31, 32, 33, 37, 39, 41, 42, 44, 56, 57, 58, 61, 62, 69, 70, 71, 76, 82, 84, 85, 86, 87, 88, 98, 101, 102, 103, 104, 122, 124, 126, 127, 131, 132, 139, 143, 146, 148, 153, 170, 179, 187, 202, 206, 207, 208, 214, 215, 216, 217*

   Chat *37*

   Credits *103*

   Places *98*

feedback *37, 51, 53, 54, 56, 83, 103, 105, 107, 108, 111, 161, 185, 186, 188, 203, 207, 208*

Flickr *42, 75, 97, 122*

AskSteve.co

Foursquare *97, 98, 122*

freelance *92, 106, 108, 109, 110, 122*

fundraising *58, 118*

G

games *21, 59, 69, 103, 107, 127, 131, 216, 217*

Gap *39*

Gmail *see* Google: Mail

Google *30, 31, 33, 61, 69, 70, 72, 77, 78, 85, 96, 104, 133, 208*

    Analytics *208*

    Docs *78*

    Google+ *30, 104*

    Mail *30, 76, 78*

    Reader *85*

    Search *30*

Gotomeeting *164*

Gotowebinar *82, 95, 122, 164, 175, 176*

Groupon *13, 33, 34, 101*

groupthink *53*

H

hacking *16, 129, 148*

Hi5 *69, 70, 102*

home entertainment *59*

I

ideas platforms *92, 118*

Incentient *74*

information brokers *46*

InnoCentive *57, 119, 122*

SocialMediaInBusiness.com

instant messaging *39, 58, 95, 103*

Instantteleseminar *82*

intranet *26, 55, 81, 85, 87, 173*

J

Jing *97*

K

keyword *30, 50*

KickApps *122*

L

Layar *75*

leadership *33, 36, 80, 138, 217*

LinkedIn *26, 31, 43, 44, 49, 50, 51, 61, 83, 84, 85, 102, 124, 127, 146, 170, 179, 202, 207, 209, 215*

local & global *26, 29, 32, 33, 56, 61, 69*

    Groupon example *33*

location services *74, 92, 97*

M

MailChimp *78*

Make.tv *99, 122*

market intelligence *92, 120, 121, 122*

marketplaces *92, 100, 101, 102, 122*

market research *30, 34, 56*

marketing *15, 29, 30, 33, 34, 56, 64, 82, 83, 86, 95, 99, 106, 116, 120, 121, 137, 140, 148, 186, 203, 205, 206, 209, 216*

media sharing *77, 92, 96*

meetings & conferencing *26, 32, 38, 39, 58, 62, 86, 92, 93, 94, 95, 104, 112, 127, 145, 155, 175, 176, 186, 204, 205*

AskSteve.co

meta tag *30*

microblogs *92, 100, 104*

Microsoft

Office Live *78*

Tags *75, 76*

milestone *158, 163, 177, 178, 179, 180, 181, 182, 203, 204, 214*

mindsets *see* culture

mitigation strategies *16, 22, 140*

mobile Internet *13, 21, 72, 74, 79, 88, 135, 217*

MSN *69, 70, 126*

MyNetFone *78*

MySpace *15, 69, 70, 88, 124*

N

Ning *44, 122*

Nokia *72*

O

Obama, Barack *50*

oDesk *110, 111, 122*

online meetings *see* virtual meetings

opt-in list *202*

organizational design *134, 135, 136*

organizational politics *81, 138, 139*

Orkut *69, 70, 102*

P

PBworks *113*

personal reputation *see* social capital

personal vs. professional life *124, 125, 126*

PEST analysis *153, 155, 172, 174*

SocialMediaInBusiness.com

Petitionbuzz *58*

petitions *58*

Photobucket *97*

pilot trial *83, 144, 150, 152, 154, 157, 158, 160, 161, 162, 163, 164, 165, 176, 182, 212, 213, 219*

Plaxo *85*

plug-in *105*

podcasting *41*

prediction platforms *see* ideas platforms

privacy *16, 98, 132, 133, 142, 145, 148, 218*

product creation *30, 83, 88*

Project Development Cycle *17, 21, 22, 23, 80, 150, 151, 155, 156, 158, 159, 160, 164, 165, 167, 168, 169, 171, 175, 176, 177, 179, 181, 182, 184, 186, 203, 204, 210, 213, 219*

   actions *157, 180, 204, 214*

   analysis *157, 171, 172, 173, 213*

   communication *157, 184, 214*

   goals *157, 169, 170, 171, 208, 213*

   measure *157, 181, 182, 184, 207, 208, 214*

   projects *157, 174, 175, 176, 213*

   strategy *157, 177, 203, 214*

project management *21, 58, 60, 78, 111, 112, 155, 159, 160, 161, 203, 207*

   briefing *152, 157, 165, 219*

   definition *152, 157*

   execution *165*

   implementation *48, 152, 159, 160, 162*

   pitfalls *22, 154, 155*

   planning *16, 140, 152, 159, 160, 165, 218*

   roll-out *152, 163, 164, 176, 213*

   stages *17, 21, 150, 151, 152, 156, 159, 165, 183*

publishing *44, 46, 133, 204, 205*

AskSteve.co

Q

Q&A sites *see* discussion sites

QQ *69, 71, 102*

QR codes *72, 75, 76, 88*

   Microsoft Tags *75, 76*

R

R&D networks *see* ideas platforms

Radio-Frequency Identification (RFID) *59*

real-life stories *see* ideas platforms

recommendation system *54*

recruitment *84*

relationship

   building *84, 89, 146*

   mapping *45*

remote training *60, 82, 88, 95, 96*

reputation management *16, 128, 148*

resourcing *84, 89, 159*

return on investment (ROI) *153, 158*

risks of social media *see* social media: dark side

RSS *113, 202, 208*

S

Salesforce *40*

Saxe, John Godfrey *23, 24*

Scribd *41*

search engine optimization (SEO) *30, 106*

search engine ranking *30, 31, 55, 69, 70, 71, 83, 120*

Search Engine Visibility *30*

SocialMediaInBusiness.com

Second Life *107, 108, 122*

security *16, 26, 60, 78, 81, 86, 124, 129, 130, 132, 135, 142, 143, 148, 150, 153, 217, 218*

six degrees of separation *48, 49*

Skype *38, 69, 78, 79, 82, 95, 101, 109, 122, 126, 204, 205*

SlideShare *41, 42, 51, 96, 202*

smartphone *43, 72, 73, 74, 75, 76, 79, 83, 126, 135, 217*

social capital *26, 28, 46, 47, 57, 83, 89*

social media

    analysis *45, 172*

    applications *16, 17, 21, 22, 23, 26, 34, 60, 91, 93, 98, 101, 108, 122, 150, 173, 176, 189, 208, 212*

    dark side *13, 16, 21, 22, 24, 89, 117, 124, 128, 140, 141, 142, 146, 148, 150, 154, 155, 157, 158, 161, 163, 179, 212, 213, 219*

    goals *17, 165, 169, 170, 171, 177, 182*

    marketing *30, 33, 106*

    networks *38, 44, 45, 46, 47, 53, 54, 67, 81, 82, 85, 86, 92, 96, 97, 100, 102, 122, 126, 127, 128, 129, 130, 131, 132, 138, 145, 173*

    platforms *15, 23, 27, 28, 29, 32, 37, 62, 64, 82, 131, 135, 139, 141, 146, 148, 217*

    policy *16, 38, 41, 43, 124, 135, 141, 142, 143, 144, 187, 188, 212, 217, 218*

    project *17, 150, 165, 170, 171, 174, 176, 181, 186, 212*

    tools *see* social media: platforms

social media networks *see* social networking

social networking *21, 26, 32, 33, 44, 47, 49, 59, 88, 102, 103, 106, 126, 137, 138, 139, 142, 143*

sourcing *84, 89, 119*

spying *see* company spying

spy-ware *16, 129, 148*

Starbucks *56, 57, 62, 170*

SWOT analysis *153, 155, 172, 174*

AskSteve.co

T

tablet computers *59, 72, 73, 74, 83, 88, 126, 135*

teleseminars *82, 205*

television *21, 66, 79, 88*

The 3-CORE Project Success System *13, 17, 21, 22, 149, 150, 159, 165*

time-outs *17, 168, 188*

training *15, 16, 21, 35, 40, 41, 42, 43, 62, 77, 82, 89, 95, 107, 144, 148, 154, 157, 160, 161, 171, 175, 176, 187, 188, 205, 207, 208, 212, 213, 217, 218, 219*

Trampoline Systems *45*

transparency *40, 47, 78, 138, 141, 185, 187*

Trendrr *120*

TripAdvisor *14, 54, 116*

TripIt *51*

trust *16, 28, 38, 53, 54, 58, 78, 81, 124, 130, 133, 145, 146, 147, 148, 218*

Twitter *21, 24, 26, 32, 33, 41, 42, 61, 69, 71, 79, 101, 105, 106, 122, 129, 135, 148, 179, 187, 202, 208, 214, 215*

TypePad *105*

U

Ustream.tv *79, 99, 122*

V

video conferencing *59, 62, 95*

viral growth *33, 34*

virtual meetings *26, 32, 58, 81, 94, 204, 205*

virtual ownership *39*

Virtual Private Network (VPN) *135*

virtual worlds *44, 92, 100, 106, 107, 108, 122*

visibility *see* Visible Market Presence

Visible Market Presence *26, 27, 28, 29, 64, 82, 83, 136*

Voice Over Internet Protocol (VoIP) *78*

W

Web 2.0 *20, 66, 67, 88*

webcasting *98, 99*

webinars *40, 82, 95, 96, 161, 175, 176, 202, 205*

Wetpaint *122*

Wii *59*

WikiLeaks *55*

Wikinews *118, 122*

Wikipedia *55, 58, 62, 69, 70, 75, 112, 118, 122*

wikis *55, 58, 60, 61, 92, 108, 112, 117, 122, 164*

Wikitude *75*

Windows Live Messenger *37, 69, 70*

WordPress *61, 105, 106, 122*

Wrike *58, 111, 122*

X

Xbox *59*

Y

Yahoo! *55, 58, 69, 70, 116, 122*
    Answers *55, 58, 116, 122*

YouTube *24, 26, 32, 40, 41, 42, 61, 62, 69, 70, 71, 79, 83, 96, 101, 122, 129, 148, 179, 202, 206, 208, 215, 217*

Z

Zoho *78, 112, 122*

AskSteve.co

Lightning Source UK Ltd.
Milton Keynes UK
UKOW050822240911

179217UK00002B/2/P

9 781908 035028